The Art
of Making Small
Wood Boxes

The Art of Making *Small* Wood Boxes

Award-Winning Designs

Tony Lydgate

Sterling Publishing Co., Inc. New York
A Sterling/Chapelle Book

For Chapelle Ltd.

Owner: Jo Packham

Editor: Karmen Potts Quinney

Staff: Marie Barber, Malissa Boatwright, Kass Burchett, Rebecca Christensen, Holly Fuller, Marilyn Goff, Michael Hannah, Shirley Heslop, Holly Hollingsworth, Susan Jorgensen, Susan Laws, Pauline Locke, Ginger Mikkelsen, Barbara Milburn, Linda Orton, Leslie Ridenour, Cindy Rooks, and Cindy Stoeckl

Photographer: Kevin Dilley • Hazen Photography Studio

Photography Stylist: Susan Laws

Exploded Diagrams: Richard Long

Library of Congress Cataloging-in-Publication Data

Lydgate, Tony.
The art of making small wood boxes : award-winning designs / Tony Lydgate.
p. cm.
"A Sterling/Chapelle book."
Includes index.
ISBN 0-8069-9576-9
1. Wooden boxes. 2. Woodwork. I. Title.
TT200.L9398 1997 97-15268
745.593-dc21 CIP

10 9 8 7 6 5 4 3 2 1

Published by Sterling Publishing Company, Inc.,
387 Park Avenue South, New York, NY 10016
© 1997 by Chapelle Limited
Distributed in Canada by Sterling Publishing
℅ Canadian Manda Group, One Atlantic Avenue, Suite 105, Toronto, Ontario, Canada M6K 3E7
Distributed in Great Britain and Europe by Cassell PLC, Wellington House, 125 Strand, London WC2R 0BB, England
Distributed in Australia by Capricorn Link (Australia) Pty Ltd., P.O. Box 6651, Baulkham Hills, Business Centre, NSW 2153, Australia
Printed and Bound in Hong Kong
All rights reserved

Sterling ISBN 0-8069-9576-9

TT200
.L9398
1997

If you have any questions or comments or would like information on specialty products featured in this book, please contact: Chapelle Ltd., Inc.
P.O. Box 9252 Ogden, UT 84409
(801) 621-2777
FAX (801) 621-2788

The written instructions, photographs, designs, patterns, and projects in this volume are intended for the personal use of the reader and may be reproduced for that purpose only. Any other use, especially commercial use, is forbidden under law without the written permission of the copyright holder. Every effort has been made to ensure that all the information in this book is accurate. However, due to differing conditions, tools, and individual skills, the publisher cannot be responsible for any injuries, losses, and other damages which may result from the use of the information in this book.

Contents

About the Author

My love of wood has its roots on islands in the Pacific and Atlantic Oceans. My family is originally from the Hawaiian island of Kauai, where Lydgate State Park is named after my grandfather. I grew up surrounded by the fabulous color, texture, and smell of woods such as koa, mango, milo, ohia, and sandalwood. As a young man transported to Martha's Vineyard, off the coast of New England, I had the great good fortune to be apprenticed to a master builder engaged in restoring eighteenth-century whaling captains' homes. These were constructed by shipwrights, many without the use of nails or other metal fasteners. I was awed by what these builders' hands had accomplished, and determined to discover what mine might do.

I turned to woodwork full-time in 1978, and over the years, my functional jewelry boxes and sculptural chests have appeared in art galleries, fine woodworking stores, and juried craft exhibitions throughout the country. I am a firm believer in the importance of giving away what I know, which has led to the many articles I have published on both the art and the business of woodwork. Fifth in a series of books I've written for Chapelle/Sterling, *The Art of Making Small Wood Boxes* has two aims: to celebrate the brilliant work of contemporary American box-makers, and to show you something about not only how, but why, people like you make beautiful things.

Photo by Judy Dater

Introduction

The handcrafted wood box is among the most intriguing of objects, and one that provides as much pleasure for the person who makes it as for the person who owns it. The woodworker creating the box experiences the challenge of design, and exercises the skills of fabrication, detailing, and finishing. The person who owns the box enjoys its visual and tactile qualities, and feels repeated delight every time the box is opened to reveal its secrets.

The Best Things Come in Small Boxes

We are affected both by the size of an object and by its scale, which refers to the visual relationships among the object, its component parts, and its surroundings. As things diminish in size and scale, from "as tall as I am," to "small enough to carry in two hands," to "so tiny it fits in the palm of my hand," our feelings about them change. The smaller the box, the greater the sense of intimacy; the smaller the box, the more irresistible becomes the impulse to touch, to hold, and to open.

To explore the pleasures of the small box, this book presents a treasury of forty box designs by thirty-one of the country's leading box-makers. These designs invite woodworkers of all skill levels, from beginner to master, to share in the delights of creating this most useful—and most appreciated—of objects. Thirty-two projects, covering everything from thumbnail-sized turnings to a set of eight nesting boxes whose largest

dimension is only one inch, are accompanied by exploded diagrams and complete how-to building instructions. A Gallery Section, with eight additional boxes, provides inspiration and stimulates the imagination with new design ideas. All projects are designed to be made in the home workshop, and are intended solely for personal use, and not for commercial manufacture or sale.

A basic rule for success in boxes of any size, as in all woodwork, is this: start where you are, with whatever tools and materials you have available. Today's woodworking magazines and tool catalogs are filled with enough fancy machinery and shiny gadgets to make any woodworker feel inadequate. Remember, however, for hundreds of years, the great masters of woodworking had no electric tools, no carbide bits, no aluminum oxide abrasives. Their masterpieces were created through elbow grease, determination, and a firm belief in the rightness of one's own way of doing things—the very attributes most home woodworkers have in abundance.

Special Techniques for Small Boxes

Despite their small scale, most of the projects in this book were made using the conventional woodworking tools and techniques described below. Several box-makers, however, have developed some special techniques.

Judy Ditmer (Tiny Turned Boxes, page 100): "I have a whole set of miniature scrapers that I've ground to size, some with left-hand and right-hand hooks. Making these extremely small turned vessels, I find I need a specialized tool for every different type of cut. In fact, it takes more tools to make these boxes than any other kind of turning I do."

Gary White (Quilt Pattern Boxes, page 40): "My work took a quantum leap forward when I switched from rulers and tape measures to calipers and micrometers. Measuring everything in thousandths of an inch, instead of in fractions, enabled me to greatly improve my accuracy. My geometric designs contain dozens of small parts; that has a big effect both on the final appearance of a box, and on how well parts go together."

Lori Glick (Painted Boxes, page 27): "I use all standard tools, but I find that with small boxes, there's a lot more hand work. I like to work in the daytime, so I get good daylight, and above all, I like to be able to spend lots of time on each piece."

Bradford Rockwell (Inch Box Set, page 60): "When people ask me how I make something as small as my Inch Box Set, the first thing I say is, 'carefully!' I use a table saw to make most of my cuts, and to keep small parts from chipping or being literally blown away by the blade, I wrap them in masking tape. I also put a strip of double-sided masking tape down on my workbench to hold small parts while I'm working on them."

Katherine Heller (Emily's Chest, page 83): "I use all the big power tools, plus a lot of hand planes and other hand tools. One thing though, sometimes doing all this close work makes me feel like a dentist."

Bonnie Klein (Ivory Box, page 121): "I use a jeweler's magnifying visor, and I've designed a small lathe and a set of turning tools for small work. The cutting theory and techniques don't change depending on the scale of what I'm doing, but it is nice to have appropriate tools."

Thom Breeze (Carved Shell and Leaf Boxes, page 38): "If you have patience, in time everything will come."

General Instructions

1. Tools

The milling operations that produced the boxes featured in this book can be performed in any number of different ways. Some operations are best done entirely by hand; for others, the appropriate power tool not only gets the job done quicker, but also more accurately and reliably.

Table Saw

The box-maker's basic tool, this machine will rip, crosscut, rabbet, resaw, dado, bevel, slot, trim, miter, and angle. A 10"-diameter blade is the most practical, and heavier-duty models are preferable because they tend to be more accurate, especially for repeated cuts. A sturdy fence, which can be used on either side of the saw blade, and an adjustable miter fence are essential accessories. Saw blades should be carbide tipped, and kept as sharp as possible. Kerf width, and number and type of teeth vary according to the particular cut to be made. Blades accumulate resin, especially when milling dense hardwoods; therefore, after every hour of use, clean them with spray-on oven cleaner.

6" x 48" Belt Sander

Sanding objects with flat surfaces is easiest on a stationary belt sander; 6" x 48" is a convenient and widely available size. Coarse grits such as 30x and 60x are useful for removing large areas of excess wood and/or glue. Medium grit belts, 120x and 150x, shape, round, and bevel, and are essential intermediate steps in the overall sanding process.

Drill Press

A drill press provides controlled drilling capability for plugs, screw holes, and invisible hinge pins. It is also useful with a sanding drum attachment, with abrasive sleeves of varying diameters, and grits.

Band Saw

The band saw is essential for resawing material wider than 6" and for curved cuts. With progressively narrower and finer-toothed blades, the band saw is the tool of choice for many machine cuts on smaller boxes.

Shaper or Router with Router Table

Many milling operations such as dadoes, round overs, and hollowing solids are best performed by either of these tools. For safe operation, as well as a wealth of applications, consult *Router Basics* and *The Router Handbook*, both by Patrick Spielman and published by Sterling.

Lathe

Some of the projects in this book, such as Judy Ditmer's Tiny Turned Vessels, page 100, and Lorenzo Freccia's Acorn Box, page 104, require the use of a lathe. Consult *The Art of the Lathe,* also by Patrick Spielman and published by Sterling.

Joiner

The joiner is important for creating a flat face on stock, as well as for removing rough surfaces.

Thickness Sander

Although not all home shops have this tool, most mills and many cabinet shops do. It is worth the effort to gain access to this tool, because it saves so much time in cleaning up surfaces, as well as in producing precisely dimensioned thicknesses.

● ● ●

No home shop, of course, has every tool. Finding ways to produce good results using only the tools and materials at hand is one of woodworking's most treasured challenges. The ingenuity bred by this challenge often leads to alternative techniques, new designs, and discoveries. In the perfectly equipped shop, where machines do all the thinking, such discoveries are rarely encountered.

Another source of innovation is the errors that even the most skilled craftsman will inevitably make. Making a nonreversible mistake forces you to rethink, to look at the situation from a new perspective. Like making do with what tools you have, this rethinking can suggest new ideas. It is said that the mark of a true master in any field is the ability to fix whatever mistakes arise. To this it should be added that a good box-maker views a mistake not as an annoying obstacle, but rather as a creative opportunity.

2. Selecting and Preparing Stock

Much of the visual impact of the projects in this book comes from the extraordinary natural beauty of their raw materials. Each project includes a list of the woods used. Highly figured hardwood is especially appropriate for small boxes because, like pearls and many gemstones, it results from natural irregularities and deformities.

An example of highly figured wood used in a box.

Much of the fun of making boxes is in creating unique and unusual wood combinations. Woodworkers are encouraged to experiment with whatever is locally available. Be certain any tropical hardwoods used are certified to come from a source that practices sustainable yield forest management. One sources for interesting woods that is often overlooked is your own backyard. Many native species that are not harvested commercially yield beautiful lumber. Moreover, grain patterns such as burl, birdseye, crotch, curly or fiddleback appear in these species as frequently as in more familiar woods. Neighbors, the highway department, tree trimming companies, even the local dump can be good sources.

To minimize the danger of damage to a finished box due to parts swelling or shifting, privately harvested lumber must be properly air-dried before it is used, and store-bought lumber should be kiln-dried.

Be aware that despite the most careful precautions, nothing is immune to the ravages of time. Finishes dull, colors fade, woods dry out, parts shift, adhesives weaken, and cracks open and close with the passing seasons. These do not detract from the beauty of a box, but rather certify that it was made by human hands using natural materials.

Although wood in any form may be used as a starting point, the most useful dimension for box-making lumber is boards of 1" or 2" thickness. Look for interesting color, grain, or figure, even if not uniformly distributed throughout the entire board.

Unlike furniture, box making—especially on a small scale—does not require large quantities of lumber; a small burl, knot, or flash of figure may be perfect for a box lid or drawer front. (The doors of the Miniature Chest by Joel Gelfand, page 114, are a good example.) Use the remaining plain part of the board for drawer sides, bottoms, or trays.

Boards are often milled before they are offered for sale. A planer is used to remove the rough exterior, allowing the natural color and grain to show more clearly, and one edge is ripped straight. This assists the buyer, but also reduces available thickness, and may make it difficult to mill certain parts out of a given board. Additionally, those piles of shavings on the sawmill floor are money—surfaced lumber costs more than the same lumber in the rough. For these reasons, lumber should be bought rough whenever possible. Box-makers should develop the ability to "read" the grain of a board when it is still rough-sawn. This skill will permit them to detect figure that a casual observer may miss.

Plywood, found in the tombs of the Egyptian Pharaohs is among the most ancient of all woodworking innovations. It is made of a series of thin solid wood laminates, glued together with the grain of each layer going in the opposite direction. Many of the projects in this book use plywood in places, such as the bottoms of boxes, drawers, and trays where dimensional stability is essential. Veneer plywoods are often used in applications where the surface will be visible.

Once rough lumber for box parts has been selected and cut to rough size or "blanked out," each piece should be given as flat a face as possible, using the belt sander or joiner. Since the irregular grain of many highly figured woods leads to chipping or tear-out on the joiner, the sander is often the only realistic alternative. With one side flat, parts can be accurately ripped to thickness. Add a hair to the final dimension to allow for finish sanding, and rip on the table saw using a push stick. If the finished piece is to be taller than about 3", the maximum cutting height of a 10" table saw blade, two passes will be needed to complete the rip cut to thickness.

Parts are then trimmed to width, again adding a bit to the dimension to allow for edge sanding. If a machine is available, this is the time to run the parts through an abrasive planer or thickness sander. This tool offers two advantages. First, it produces parts that are uniform and precisely dimensioned, and second, it accomplishes the initial step in the sanding process, accurately laying down parallel grooves of equal depth on the surface of the wood. Parts that have been deliberately milled slightly thicker and wider are quickly brought down to precise final dimension by repeated passes through this machine. Dimensioned and sanded parts are now ready for the slots, rabbets, dadoes, or holes that will later facilitate assembly of bottoms, rails, and dowels.

3. Milling

In box-making, more than in any other type of woodworking, milling and assembly alternate in the sequence of fabrication steps leading to the final product. Dimensioned parts are glued together, and the resulting assembly is then remilled in preparation for yet another assembly. This back-and-forth process may be repeated several times.

Each of the projects in this book includes a list of parts and their dimensions. Since the process of box making is not an exact science, it is important not to cut every part in a project to listed finish dimensions before beginning box assembly. When making a project with drawers, for example, a box-maker may decide to use a particularly nice piece of wood that might be thinner or thicker than the one diagrammed. As a result, the actual length of the drawer front and back may vary. Furthermore, parts with close tolerances, such as lids and drawers, generally have to be hand fitted. The best approach is to make the box body first, then dimension and fabricate lids and drawers.

Finally, milling small pieces of wood can be awkward. Parts that will end up shorter than about 10" should be prepared "two up" whenever practical. Perform all dimensioning, slotting, and preassembly sanding operations on this longer, easier-to-handle stock, and crosscut to final size just prior to mitering.

The Miter Joint

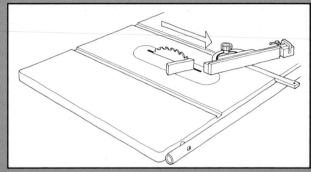

Diagram A

One of the most versatile means of joining box parts, the miter appears in many of the projects in this book. It produces a joint that is neat in appearance, does not show end grain, and can easily be reinforced with splines or slipfeathers. The secret to successful miters is accurate milling. Make certain the angles of both the table saw blade and the miter fence can be accurately set and precisely maintained. For miters on stock less than 3" wide, set the miter fence at a 45 degree angle and mill the workpiece standing on its edge (see Diagram A above). For miters on wider stock, set the table saw blade at 45 degrees, return the miter fence to a right angle, and lay the workpiece on its face (see Diagram B on facing page). In either case, make trial cuts on scrap pieces first, to ensure miter settings are as accurate as available tools will permit.

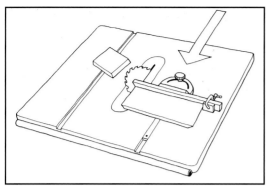

Diagram B

Slipfeathers

The slipfeathers used in several of the projects in this book (see Timothy Lydgate's Inlaid Boxes, page 63) are triangular wedges glued into saw kerfs milled horizontally in the corners of a box, lid, or other part. Slip-feathers serve to mechanically reinforce the adhesive bond in a joint, and also provide a strong visual element. They are made by passing a part or assembly over the table saw blade on a carrier block. The workpiece sits on edge in a 90 degree V-groove cut into this block (see Diagram C below). (In its simplest form, a slipfeather block can be made from a 12" length of two-by-four.) The number, depth, and placement of slipfeathers vary with the design, and their thickness is determined by the kerf width.

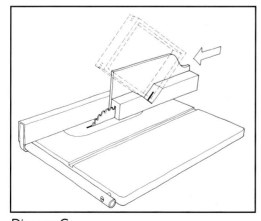

Diagram C

Trays and Dividers

A velvet-lined tray is a useful feature of many box designs. An elegant but practical version, adaptable to a wide variety of sizes and shapes, is shown in Diagram D.

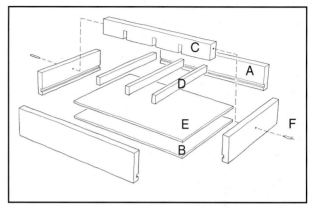

Diagram D

Stock for sides (Part A) is given a shallow saw kerf dado to receive the tray bottom. The joints may be butted as shown, mitered, or rabbeted. Eighth-inch veneer plywood with one hardwood face (Part B) is used for the bottom. The finished tray may be divided into any number of compartments. For dividers, saw kerfs are cut into the underside of a rectangular rail (Part C) that exactly fits inside the tray. Small divider strips ⅛" thick (Part D), their top edges rounded on the sander, are then glued into the kerfs. After it is dry from oiling, the divider is placed in the tray atop the velvet pad (Part E). Pins (Part F) driven partway through the sides of the tray into the ends of the long rail hold the divider firmly in place. These may be countersunk; the holes filled with small dowels, and sanded flush.

Velvet Linings

A simple procedure for lining boxes and trays is to wrap material such as velvet or suede over pieces of posterboard or matte board, which are cut about ⅟₁₆" smaller than the space to be lined. (Exact dimensions of the matte board will vary with the thickness of the lining material.) Make this material $\frac{1}{2}$" wider all around than the matte board, and attach with spray adhesive. For neat corners, use a sharp blade to cut off triangular sections, then apply more adhesive, and fold down the material (see Diagram E). The completed pad should jam in place tightly enough to stay put, but not so tightly that the matte board buckles.

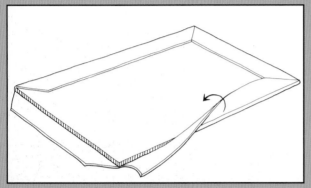

Diagram E

Slicing Off the Lid

In some box designs, like those by Ed Love (page 67), it is important to maintain the continuity of the grain pattern from the body of the box to the lid. To achieve this, box and lid are glued as a single unit, and the lid is later separated by ripping on the table saw. In addition to preserving continuous grain, this approach has the advantage of eliminating the need to mill separate parts for body and the lid, and go through two gluing operations. One caution: in sizing parts, remember that the saw kerf, plus follow-up sanding, will consume anywhere from $\frac{1}{16}$" to $\frac{3}{16}$" of material, so dimension the four sides accordingly.

To separate the lid using the table saw, set the blade to a height no more than $\frac{1}{8}$" greater than the thickness of the box side. After

ensuring that there are no blobs of glue or other interferences between the top of the box and the table saw fence, rip one long side, then each of the two short sides. Make certain the box is held steady as it passes over the blade: any wiggle will require large amounts of sanding later on to restore uniform flatness to the ripped surfaces.

Natural stresses built into the box during gluing may be released when the fourth and final cut is made. To protect against any pinching this might cause, insert a filler before making the fourth cut. Use a scrap piece of $\frac{1}{8}$" plywood or similar material that is as wide as the cut is deep, as shown in Diagram F. Attach the plywood to a stop block; this allows the filler assembly to rest securely on the top of the box during the cut.

Since vibrator or pad sanders can inadvertently round-over edges, use a hand sanding block with progressively finer grit sandpaper to clean up the saw blade marks on the edges of the sides after the lid has been separated. Despite these precautionary measures, however, it requires special care to ensure that the surfaces remain flat, especially at the corners.

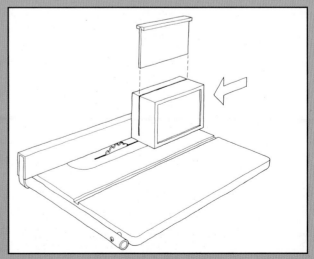

Diagram F

Laminates

Thin strips of differing woods are often laminated or glued together for decorative effect. Since laminated parts are often resawn and recombined with other parts, as in the lid of the Credit Card Box by Bradford Rockwell (page 58), they must be precisely dimensioned. This means that great care must be taken in milling the strips. Make certain that the stock from which the strips are cut is uniform, and that its edge is always a perfect 90 degrees.

Gluing up a laminate requires a "sandwich" clamping jig, as shown in Diagram G. Use scrap ¾" plywood to make a base plate (Part A) that is about 4" wider and 2" longer than the laminate assembly (Part F). Also, make two clamping rails (Part B), each about 2" wide, and two sandwich blocks (Part C), each about as long as the width of the assembly. One set of clamps (Part D), glues the laminates together. A second set (Part E) keeps the assembly being glued from buckling by sandwiching it between blocks clamped on either end.

To avoid gluing the clamping blocks to the laminate—or the laminate to the base plate—line each with a single sheet of newspaper (Part G). The glue won't penetrate the newspaper, which means that when it is dry and the clamps are removed, everything should come apart easily. Any glued-on newspaper is then sanded off, along with excess glue.

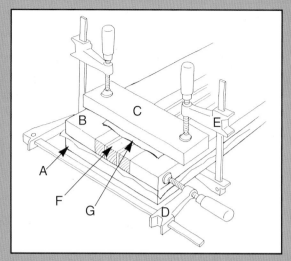

Diagram G

Invisible Hinge Pins

The lids of the Quilt Pattern Boxes designed by Gary White (page 40) and others operate with an invisible pin hinge. This mechanism has a number of advantages: it is relatively straightforward to assemble and requires no elaborate hardware. More importantly, the lid can be made separately, and when installed lies flush with the top edges of the box.

Parts for the lid should be dimensioned to make an exact fit with the size of the box opening. After the lid is assembled, it is fitted to the opening by sanding on the edge using the 6" x 48" belt sander with a sharp fine grit belt, such as 150x. Be certain to allow sufficient operating clearance, especially along the rear edge. The lid must then be held securely in place while pilot holes are drilled for the hinge pins.

To do this, place small strips of newspaper in the gaps between the lid and the box sides, then jam the lid in place with reasonable (but not excessive) hand pressure. Depending on the size of the gap, a thickness of four or five pieces of newspaper usually suffices. Next, mark the sides of the box for the hinge pins.

Vertically, these marks should be centered relative to the the thickness of the lid. If the lid is ½" thick, mark them at ¼" down from the upper surface of the box sides. Horizontally, they are located ¼" plus 1/16" from the inside face of the box back. This extra 1/16" allows the lid, when opened, to come to rest against the box back at the desired angle: ten to fifteen degrees past vertical.

Use a drill press to drill pilot holes for the hinge pins on these marks. A brass pin or 4d or 6d finish nail works well as the hinge pin; size the drill bit accordingly. After drilling, remove the newspaper wedges, and make certain all lid surfaces are finish sanded. Then install the lid with the hinge pins, as shown in Diagram H, below. The point of each pin should bite slightly into the lid, and the end should terminate about 1/8" inside the outer face of the box sides. (If using a finish nail, remove the head with nippers). To plug holes and cover end of pins, glue in a short length of dowel of the same wood as the box, handmade on the 6" x 48" belt sander. When the glue is dry, sand off any excess length.

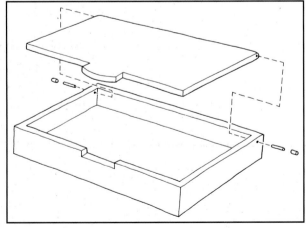

Diagram H

4. Sanding

The most important element in the look of a finished box is the shape and feel of its finished surfaces, and sanding is the operation that produces them. Before this point, abrasive treatments play an important role in shaping forms, and creating round overs and eased radii.

To abrade is to scratch, and abrasives such as sandpaper do literally that. Consisting of a jumble of tiny rocks glued to a paper or cloth backing, they carve into the wood a pattern of grooves, like furrows plowed into a field. When a belt sander is used, these grooves are parallel and of uniform depth. How deep is determined by the grit rating of the abrasive: as this number increases, groove depth decreases. A perfect finish is produced by repeated sanding with progressively finer grits, making these parallel grooves shallower and shallower until they become invisible.

The importance of an orderly sequence of grits cannot be overemphasized. Too broad a leap, such as going from coarse to very fine with nothing in between, will prove unsatisfactory. An attempt to remove 60x scratches with a 220x abrasive will simply produce well-sanded scratches; the 220x rocks are too small to obliterate the grooves the 60x rocks have made. When the 60x is followed by 120x, then 180x, and then 220x, however, the result will be a smooth surface.

The flat platen of the belt sander is not useful for most curved or irregular shapes; the best means for bringing such surfaces to the desired finish is hand or orbital sanding. Caution must be used with orbital sanders, however; they occasionally leave circular scratches when crossing the grain, and can produce unintended round overs as the pad passes over the edge of a workpiece. Hand sanding is always the best method. The more irregular the shape, and the harder the wood, the more time and effort will be needed to achieve a good finish.

Whatever tools are used, the sanding process should be frequently interrupted to check the work with that best of all tools, the eye. A useful procedure for determining the exact condition of a surface is as follows. Hold the part in one hand and extend the arm. Using a window, skylight, or light bulb, make a straight line between the eyeball, the surface to be inspected, and the light source (see Diagram J).

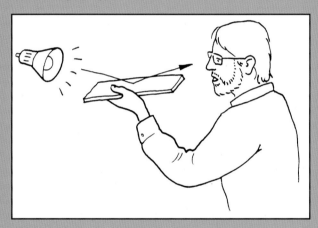

Diagram J

Adjust the position of the hand until the angles are just right, and the light will pick up every detail of the surface, showing even the tiniest scratches. When this extended-arm inspection no longer reveals any defects, the polishing process is complete, and the piece is ready for its liquid finish.

Other Sanding Operations

In designs such as William Chappelow's Double Ladle Box (page 96), some box parts must be literally sculpted out of a block of solid wood. A moving abrasive belt, drum, or sleeve is often the most effective way to do this, especially if the shape is irregular or curved. Routers, carving tools, shapers, and band saws may also be used, but these leave rough surfaces that will require additional sanding prior to finish. Further-more, any cutting tool used with figured hardwoods presents the risk of chipping and tear out.

Many boxes have flat sides that meet at crisp mitered corners. When these corners are too crisp, however, their edges are so sharp they are uncomfortable to handle. More important, a too-sharp edge will also inevitably collect tiny dings and dents, every one of which will be clearly visible. To prevent this, the sharp edges of a box should be lightly sanded or "edge-killed" by hand prior to final finish.

In some designs, the top edges of a box are to be rounded over. The desired curve is not a true radius, but somewhere halfway between that and a 90 degree angle, and is referred to as an "eased radius". This type of edge treatment makes the finished product both more durable and more pleasing to the eye. It can be produced with a handheld orbital sander, or on the belt sander by holding the box firmly in both hands, and rocking the edge back and forth over the moving belt, grain parallel to the direction of rotation.

Where a true radius is desired, the belt sander quickly and efficiently removes the slight tool marks that even the sharpest carbide bit will leave. In many cases, there is no need to sand outside surfaces prior to assembly, especially when they are flat. Sanding after glue-up will smooth the outside surfaces, remove excess glue, grind slipfeathers or laminates flush, and correct any irregularities of rectilinearity or form, all in the same operation.

5. Assembly

A useful technique is to approach a new project as an exploration. Before attempting a definitive version of a given design, make one or two experimental runs, using trial materials such as softwood, scrap plywood, or particle board, to assess the usefulness of milling and fabrication techniques, as well as the dimensions and proportion of parts. This is especially important in complex designs.

For most of the boxes in this book, inside surfaces should be sanded to finish-ready condition prior to assembly, as it is usually impossible to do so afterwards.

Before starting to glue an assembly, it is always a good idea to go through a dry run, putting all the parts together first without the adhesive. This is particularly important with more complex assemblies. The dry run not only tests for fit, but also serves as a rehearsal of the assembly process, alerting the box-maker to potential problems that may arise during time-sensitive glue-up.

Another useful practice is to test every assembly for square, plumb, or true immediately after gluing, before it becomes too late to make adjustments.

Clamping

C-clamps or other screw-type mechanical clamps are essential when substantial pressure is required, as when gluing laminate strips.

They are not widely used in box making, however, because the small scale of most box assemblies simply does not require that much force. What clamping does is hold the faces of a joint firmly together until the adhesive sets. For boxes, the most effective way to do this is usually with paper or cloth tape.

Adhesives

Aliphatic, or "white" glue, a convenient and economical adhesive, is appropriate for most projects. Epoxy, cyanoacrilate, and various types of waterproof glue can also be used. Glue should completely cover surfaces to be joined. In general, too much glue is preferable to too little: a slight squeeze of excess is evidence that there is sufficient glue to hold the joint securely. Remember, however, that this excess will be rock hard by the next day, and difficult to remove without marring a carefully polished interior. To avoid this, let the glue dry until it reaches the consistency of stiff chewing gum. This requires an hour or so, depending on the type of glue and the temperature. The excess may now be safely removed using a sharp chisel. To prevent unwanted bonding—such as gluing the box to the worktable, or the laminate strips to the clamping jig—use a single sheet of newspaper as a liner or separator. Despite its thinness, the newspaper will not be penetrated by the glue, and when dry, everything can be neatly sanded off.

No matter how carefully they are made, the joints in any project may show tiny gaps or voids; these must be filled prior to final sanding. Commercial wood fillers are available, but their colors are never quite right, especially when unusual or home-grown woods are used. A custom-made filler or "goop" is a better alternative.

Apply a scrap piece of the wood to be matched to the belt sander and carefully collect the resulting fine dust. Mix this with glue, and force the mixture into the gaps with the flat blade of an old chisel. Experiment to determine the proper consistency. If the proportion of glue to dust is too great, the result will be runny, and when dry will appear as a glue line, which does not take a satisfactory finish. If the proportion is too little, the goop will be difficult to apply and will dry rough.

6. Finishing

Once the right wood has been selected, all that is required to bring out the natural beauty of the wood is the proper surface preparation. Obtaining a beautiful finish has almost nothing to do with the product being used, and almost everything to do with the preparation of the surface to which it is applied. The deep, silken liquid look of a perfect finish, with the feeling of being able to see right down into the wood, comes not from obscure ingredients or rare compounds, but from time and elbow grease.

Two general types of clear finish are used in the projects in this book: penetrating oil, which soaks into the wood and then hardens, and lacquer or varnish, which lies on top of it. Unlike a dining table, small boxes are not designed to come in contact with water, so varnish, with its water-resistant properties, is not needed. Lacquer's quick drying time makes it easier to work with than varnish, but lacquer is not as durable nor as water resistant. Furthermore, its thinner nature means that more coats are needed to produce a satisfactory finish.

Penetrating oil finishes show off dramatic figure and grain patterns better than lacquer or varnish, whose multiple coats covering the surface tend to fill the pores of the wood. Oil finishes are relatively simple to apply, and have the advantage of not requiring a dust-free environment. Oil can be applied with a cloth, and rubbed in with fine steel wool. When the surface is dry, steel wool is again used to smooth it. The final step is to apply an appropriate wax, which is then rubbed to high luster by hand or with a buffing wheel.

7. Safety

Woodworking is inherently dangerous. The raw material itself can be heavy, sharp-edged, and splintery. The tools used to fabricate it are all potentially lethal. These factors, combined with noxious dust, harmful chemicals, high noise levels, and large quantities of electricity, produce an environment in which disfiguring, crippling, or even fatal injury can occur in dozens of unforeseen ways. To operate a safe woodshop, always keep this in mind.

The risk of injury can never be completely removed, but it can be reduced to an acceptable level by strict observation of certain guidelines.

• For safe operation of all tools, fully understand and adhere to the manufacturer's instructions.

• Never allow fingers to come near any moving blade or cutter. Use a push stick.

• Always wear a respirator or dust mask in the shop. Always wear ear and eye protection when using power tools.

• Always wear appropriate clothing. A heavy work apron will protect the midsection from occasional table saw kickback. A dropped chisel hurts less on a protected toe than on a bare one—do not wear sandals in the shop.

• Never perform any operation without being satisfied that you understand it and are comfortable with it.

• Keep your mind on your work. Do not allow your attention to wander, especially when performing repetitive operations.

• Never work when tired, in a hurry, or simply not in the mood to work. It is better to stop, or find something to do outside the shop for a while. Return refreshed and in the proper frame of mind.

Chapter One: Projects

Doug Muscanell & Karen Harbaugh

Photo by Richard Abarno

In the 1980's, following a degree in forestry and a successful career as a project engineer for a major log home builder, Doug Muscanell began handcrafting containers from ironwood and other native species in his Colorado studio. "I've always loved boxes and beautiful woods," Doug writes, "and my first experiments were built from my dad's scrap pile."

"Doug is the main technician in our woodworking operation," observes Karen Harbaugh, Doug's wife. "He has more of an eye for how the natural features of a certain piece of wood expand or limit its possibilities. I have more of a mental picture of how the finished product should look. We work really well together making small changes back and forth until we're both pleased with the result."

Karen was a social worker when she and Doug first met. "I was fascinated that someone could make a living doing this kind of work," she remembers. "When I first started working in the shop with Doug, I really appreciated the sense of accomplishment that I got from making

something tangible. Now I do most of the finish work, which has a meditative quality I like, and I handle the people part of the business.

"Our dream is to collaborate on larger, one-of-a-kind pieces. There's this huge burled ironwood log we've been saving, and every time we walk by it, one or the other of us has a new idea about what it could become."

Ironwood Freeform Boxes

Photo on page 21.

These gem-like boxes are made from chunks of desert ironwood. Doug and Karen carefully select pieces that have an organic, free-form shape. They particularly prize the pieces with sapwood, bark, and other naturally occurring irregularities. Their design is ideal for any interesting piece of wood that seems to be too small or too ornery for any other use.

Ironwood Freeform Boxes close-up

Dimensions will vary depending on the piece of wood used.

• Rough-cut the stock to approximate final dimensions, and scrape away the excess bark and dead or insect damaged wood.
• Following the instructions on page 14, slice off the lid, about ¼" thick, on the band saw. Using a router, hollow out the interior.
•Sand and polish until smooth.
•Set two ¹⁄₁₆"-diameter brass pins into the top surface of the box. These should make a precise fit with holes drilled in lid, to maintain the original profile of the stock when the box is closed. Sand and polish the exterior, leaving natural irregularities where possible.

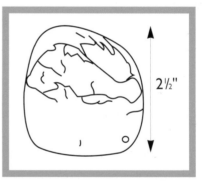

2½"

Some days I envy craft makers who work in plastic media such as clay, metal, glass, or wax, because they are free to do as they please. I mean plastic in the old sense of the word: *formable, malleable, the material does what you want it to do.* Wood, in contrast, has a mind of its own. Wood never lets you forget that it starts out as a finished product. *I have already been fabricated,* wood says to us, *by a better Maker than you.*

—T.L.

Janis Allen

Photo by Boldman

The wood of the avocado tree is so soft—as well as so difficult to come by—that few boxmakers would consider using it. On the Big Island of Hawaii, however, Janis Allen has perfected a technique for producing spalted avocado with colors and grain patterns as beautiful as they are rare.

"I taught art history in California for many years," says Janis, "but after Proposition 13 passed, teaching jobs dried up, and I decided I wanted something to do where I didn't have deadlines. I took up cabinetmaking, and one day when I needed an odd-sized piece of wood, I went out to the woodpile. Since at the time, I was part caretaker of an avocado grove, that's what was in the woodpile, and I started working with it.

"Not long afterward, my husband and I moved to Hawaii, where avocados are plentiful. Between homeowners wanting an old tree removed, and coffee plantations clearing land to plant more coffee, we found plenty of trees, some as big as three feet in diameter. We live on the west slope of Mauna Kea, and when you get up to about 2000 feet elevation, it's cool and quite wet. We toss the logs into the weeds, where the bugs and the rot will get to them, and leave them there until they turn spalted and develop these marvellous colors. If we don't get them at the right time, of course, they just rot away.

"As Hawaiian woods go, a lot of people like koa, but if I had to work with koa all the time I'd get bored. I'm absolutely fascinated by this spalted avocado. There's such variation in the wood. Every piece is so different."

Nesting Avocado Wood Boxes
Photo on page 24.

These avocado wood boxes are made from lumber that has been deliberately exposed to moisture and insects. The distinctive black lines, called spalting, are produced by a fungus. Borer beetles, termites, and other insects create tunnels and honeycomb patterns. *Note: These are freeform shapes, determined by the size of the logs at hand. The dimensions will vary depending on the particular piece of wood used.*

The photographs show two different shapes of Janis's Nesting Avocado Wood Boxes, one square, and one rectangle. The rectangle box at the top of the photographs is the smallest of its three box set, the largest of which, measuring $3\frac{7}{8}$" x $4\frac{1}{2}$" x 6", is not shown.

25

• To make this set, begin by roughing out a 5"-long section of the log that is approximately 4" by 6". Using the band saw, cut a ½"-thick slice off the top. This will become the lid of the largest box.

• Next, with the grain direction parallel to band saw blade, cut into the side of the work piece.

• Hollow out the center of the box, leaving the exterior walls about ½" thick.

• Cut a ¼" slice off the top and the bottom of resulting core. These will make the bottom and the lid liner of the largest box.

• Repeat this process for the mid-size and smallest boxes, progressively reducing the thickness of the exterior wall, bottom, and lid.

• Clamp and glue each box body to hide the vertical cut made by the band saw blade. Glue on the bottoms. Polish the lower surface of the lid liner, then glue it to the underside of the lid. Place each lid on its box, and sand the exterior. Oil, wax, and buff. Line each box

3"

Nesting Avocado Wood Boxes open

Lori Glick

"My dad was in the Air Force, so when I was growing up we moved around a lot. I've always loved to create, and from as far back as I can remember, I wanted to become an artist. I've always had very strong beliefs about how I want things to look. Maybe the fact that my external world changed so frequently contributed to my aesthetic sensitivity."

Lori Glick drew and painted all through elementary and high school, then studied weaving, ceramics, photography, and finally woodworking in college. "I decided that teaching art wasn't for me, so I needed a creative medium in which I could earn my own living," she recalls in her Northern California studio. "At first, I was intimidated by woodwork. This was fifteen years ago, at a time when you just didn't see women in the workshop. Everything was brand new, and it was pretty scary. I cried a lot.

"Fortunately I had great friends and great teachers, a wood-turning professor with the ability to make what he was doing really exciting, and a fellow student who suggested we start selling our work at local craft fairs. Now that I've gotten myself established, I can't imagine doing anything else.

"The kind of person I am doesn't leave me with much choice. I have to be creative. I feel so rewarded at the end of the day, knowing I've made something completely new, that wouldn't have come into being without me— particularly when it started out as some raggedy old board. With every box I finish, I feel like part of my soul is in it."

Painted Boxes

Photo on page 27. Exploded diagram on page 29.

• Start with a ½"-thick piece of clear pine or other soft wood 2⅛" wide and a little more than 13" long. Using two cuts on the table saw, mill a ¼" x ¾" rabbet in one edge of the stock, over which the lid will fit. On the lower edge of the opposite face, mill a ¼" dado for the bottom. Following instructions for The Miter Joint on page 12, crosscut the stock into four pieces, each a little more than 3⅛" long, and miter to final size.

• Mill the top panel and lid sides, which are put together with simple butt joints. Two small brads are nailed through each of the long sides to reinforce the attachment of the lid top panel.

• Make a trial assembly of the lid, using masking tape, and test its fit on the base. Sand to adjust as necessary. Then assemble the base and the lid.

• To carve the lid handle, start by roughing out the shape using a scroll saw or jig saw, then finish with carving chisels, rasps, and sandpaper. The decorative cutouts on the sides are made with the jig saw.

• The interesting, muted colors of these boxes are created using latex spray paint. Experiment on a scrap piece of wood, spraying a color, then partially sanding it off, and adding another color. The layers of the sanded pigment combine to produce new colors.

• After the box is painted to the desired color, rub it with newspaper. This will dull the colors slightly, as well as polish the box. Drill a pilot hole in the lid panel for the lid handle screw, then attach it.

Painted Box Lid close-up

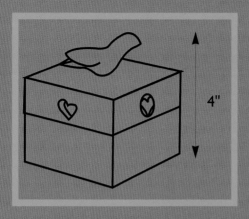

Part	Description	Dimensions	Qty
A	Side	$\frac{1}{2}$" x $2\frac{1}{8}$" x $3\frac{1}{8}$"	4
B	Bottom	$\frac{1}{8}$" x $2\frac{5}{8}$" x $2\frac{5}{8}$"	1
C	Lid top panel	$\frac{1}{4}$" x $2\frac{5}{8}$" x $2\frac{5}{8}$"	1
D	Lid side	$\frac{1}{4}$" x 1" x $3\frac{1}{8}$"	2
E	Lid side	$\frac{1}{4}$" x 1" x $2\frac{5}{8}$"	2
F	Carved handle	$\frac{5}{8}$" x 1" x $2\frac{1}{4}$"	1
G	Attachment screw	#6 x $\frac{1}{2}$"	1

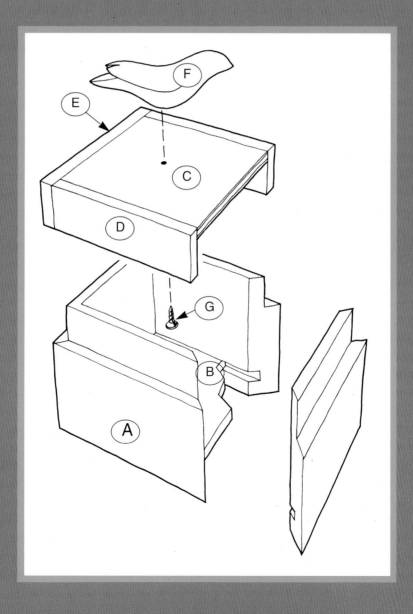

Russus Larson

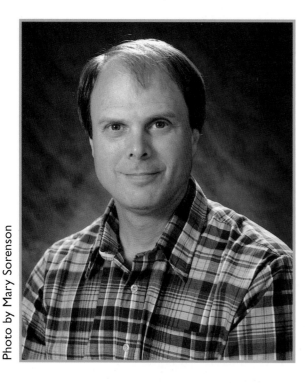

On his family farm in rural Nebraska, Russ Larson divides his time into an enviable combination of pursuits. During farming months, he raises corn and soybeans. In the winter, he's free to enjoy his passion for fine woodworking, along with teaching classes in Tae Kwan Do, and running an outboard motor sales and repair operation.

Through his woodworking business, The Wooden Gem, Russ produces custom-ordered guitars, banjos, dulcimers, chairs, cabinets, chests, hourglasses, and jewelry, in addition to the playing card boxes shown here. He developed his skills while earning a forestry degree in wood products management from the University of Missouri.

"In 1979, when I finished school, I thought for a while about working in a sawmill. But I love exotic woods, and I realized that what I really wanted to do was run the farm and start my own woodworking business.

"I prefer to design everything I make. Even on my musical instruments, the designs are my own. I did a lot of research, then decided which were the best characteristics to incorporate. I try to visualize what I want, and then I trace it out on paper to get the proportions right. Making the jigs and fixtures is the real work."

Playing Card Boxes

Photo on page 30. Exploded diagram on page 33.

These colorful and highly useful boxes for playing cards were made from Himalayan ebony, African vermilion, and osage orange (also called hedge apple or bodark).

• Start by milling ¼"-thick stock about 3" wide and 17" long. This stock should be sanded to about 220X on both faces. Crosscut the stock to make the front and the back (Part A), as well as Parts B, C and D, and trim each to final size.
• To make the decorative detailing on the front and the sides, use a router bit mounted on the drill press. The quarter-moon detail is made by first drilling a ⅝"-diameter hole on the front, then filling it by gluing in a ⅝"-diameter piece of contrasting wood (satinwood was used in the example shown). Once this is dry, drill a second ⅝"-diameter hole, slightly offset from the center of the first hole, and fill it with a circle of the same wood as the rest of the front. The stars are

short lengths of sterling silver wire, epoxied into holes drilled with the drill press.

• To make the latch mechanism, use a band saw with a narrow, fine-tooth blade to cut a ¼" x ¼" slot on the top edge of the front (Part A), and on the long edge of the lid (Part D). The latch (Part E) is a ¼" x ¼"x ½" block of wood that is glued into the slot in Part A. When the box is closed, a groove in Part E holds the brass pin (Part F) on the hinged lid. Use the band saw to cut this groove just a hair thinner than the diameter of the brass pin.

• Widen the end of the groove by making a hole with a drill bit the same diameter as the brass pin.

• Drill a hole for the latch pin in its slot in the lid. Install pin. Drill holes for the hinge pins about ½" deep into edges of the lid (Part D). The diameter of all these holes should be such that the pins will stay in them with a jam fit. On the inside faces of the sides (Part B), drill the same diameter holes part way through the stock. *Note: The holes do not go all the way through. Pins are not visible from the outside of the box. They are installed at the same time the*

Playing Card Box close-up

entire box is assembled. Round-over the inside edge of the lid to allow it to clear the back as it closes.

• Using masking tape, make a trial assembly of the box parts to test for fit. Make certain there is adequate interior clearance for a standard-sized deck of playing cards. Check to be certain all parts are properly sanded on their inside faces, and assemble with glue. After the glue is dry, sand the box lightly to smooth its exterior.

• Avoid excessive sanding on the front, as this may affect the appearance of the router bit detailing. If the latch mechanism is too tight, use a small file to adjust fit. Apply a hand-rubbed oil finish and wax.

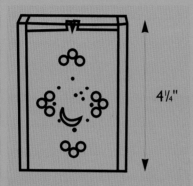

Part	Description	Dimensions	Qty
A	Front/back	$\frac{1}{4}$" x $2\frac{5}{8}$" x 4"	2
B	Side	$\frac{1}{4}$" x $1\frac{3}{16}$" x $4\frac{1}{4}$"	2
C	Base	$\frac{1}{4}$" x $1\frac{1}{16}$" x $2\frac{5}{8}$"	1
D	Lid	$\frac{1}{4}$" x $1\frac{3}{16}$" x $2\frac{5}{8}$"	1
E	Latch block	$\frac{1}{4}$" x $\frac{1}{4}$" x $\frac{1}{2}$"	1
F	Brass pin	$\frac{1}{16}$" x $\frac{1}{2}$"	3

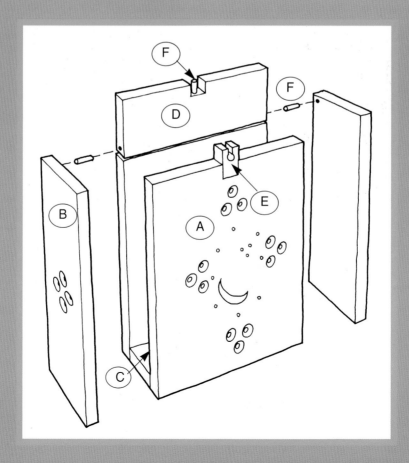

Michael Moore

Photo by Danyel Basham

Trained as a geologist, Michael Moore recently returned from a two month stint as part of the scientific crew aboard a deep sea research ship. "I was on an expedition funded by the National Science Foundation to take core samples of the Earth's crust along the ocean floor. Every once in a while my woodworking gets interrupted for a trip like this."

The rest of the year, Michael and his family live in Bastrop, Texas, just outside Austin. Bastrop is a turn-of-the-century town that has had the good fortune to preserve its original buildings. "When I'm not at sea or making boxes," Michael says, "I'm working on restoring one of these old homes."

Michael's boxes are made from mesquite, a species common throughout the southwest. "The local ranchers don't like their cattle eating mesquite, because it's so full of thorns. I have a friend who mills the lumber into flooring, and I take the pieces he rejects because of cracks or wormholes. My turquoise also comes from scraps and shards the jewelers discard. Except for the ziricote I buy to make my hinges, pretty much everything I use is recycled."

Michael credits *The Art of Making Elegant Wood Boxes*, first in this series of box-making books, with giving him the inspiration to become a woodworker.

Dovetailed Mesquite and Turquoise Boxes

Photo on page 34. Exploded diagram on page 37.

Michael Moore carefully selects pieces of mesquite with cracks or wormholes that will be filled with turquoise. (This design can be made from any species of wood that includes similar defects). The box is glued up as a single rectangular solid, with top and bottom in place, and then sliced to remove the lid.

• Prepare ½"-thick stock 2" wide by about 15" long. Crosscut the four sides to length, and mill dovetails by hand or with a router jig. Finish-sand the interior surfaces, and glue-up the four sides and the bottom. Glue on the lid top panel (Part H). Following the instructions on page 14, slice off the lid when the glue is dry.
• Prepare the box body liner strip (Part D and

35

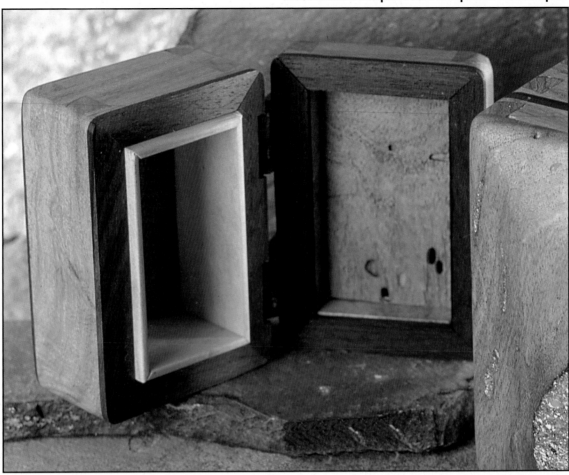

Part E), and the lid liner strip (Part J and Part K; all are made of ziricote in the example shown), and glue them to the edges of the box and lid.

• Rough-sand the exterior surfaces of the box, and then fill any cracks, wormholes, or other voids with turquoise dust mixed with clear epoxy. Use vise grip pliers, a mortar and pestle, or other grinding technique to reduce turquoise chips to appropriate size. Mill, sand, and install a ⅛"-thick liner of cherry wood (not shown in drawing) in the body of the box. This will ensure proper alignment for the lid, and cover the interior surfaces.

• Shape and finish-sand all exterior surfaces. Using a band saw, mill the hinges (Part L, Part M, and Part N) and drill holes for the hinge pin. Assemble each hinge, and carefully glue it in place. When the glue is dry, give the box a hand-rubbed oil finish.

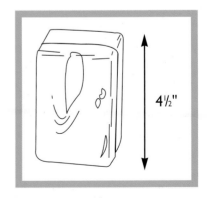

4½"

Part	Description	Dimensions	Qty
A	Box front/back	2" x 1⅜" x 4½"	2
B	Box side	2" x 1⅜" x 2⅝"	2
C	Box bottom	⅛" x 2⅛" x 3¾"	1
D	Box body liner strip*	⅛" x ½" x 2⅞"	2
E	Box body liner strip*	⅛" x ½" x 4½"	2
F	Lid front/back	½" x ½" x 4½"	2

G	Lid side	½" x ½" x 2⅝"	2
H	Lid top panel	½" x 2⅞" x 4½"	1
J	Lid liner strip	⅛" x ½" x 2⅞"	2
K	Lid liner strip	⅛" x ½" x 4½"	2
L	Upper hinge	3/16" x ¾" x 1"	2
M	Lower hinge	3/16" x ¾" x 1¼"	2
N	Wood hinge pin	⅛" x ¾"	2
O	Box liner*	⅛" x 1½" x 3½"	2
P	Box liner*	⅛" x 1½" x 1⅝"	

* not drawn

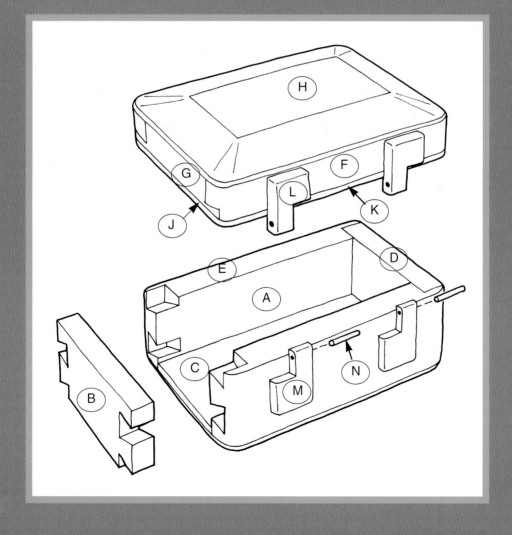

Thom Breeze

"I've always been curious about how things go together," writes Thom Breeze from his woodworking studio on the Big Island of Hawaii. When he was five, growing up on a farm in rural Illinois, Thom remembers rewiring a lamp. "That experiment blew out all the circuits on the property, but I didn't give up. As a kid, tinkering and making things became my way of keeping out of mischief. All through high school, if you wanted to find me, you'd look in the photography darkroom or the model-making shop."

Thom is one of those individuals who is fortunate to be naturally handy. "I love to create things, and technical ability has always been second nature to me. I can't entirely explain it, but I seem to know how to use tools, how things want to go together, and how far you can take a certain material before it will break. I also really like sharing my skills with other people. As a kid, I'd see something that needed fixing at a neighbor's house, and I'd go across the street and say, 'Let me fix that for you.'"

After moving to Hawaii, Thom worked as a finish carpenter in the home building industry before starting his own woodworking business. "I believe that everyone has some ability as an artist. The important thing is to develop whatever ability you possess, to motivate yourself to build on what you have, and most of all, to be patient. If you have patience, in time everything will come.

"The inspiration for the boxes I'm making now has come from two sources: encouragement from people who respected me and took an interest in my work, and the beautiful forms of nature, such as the antherium flower, the hibiscus, marine shells, and the plant called 'Bird of Paradise'. Being part of the circle, being able to do what I want, I'm one of the most fortunate people I know."

Carved Shell and Leaf Boxes

Photo on page 38.

These small carved shell and leaf boxes are made from koa. The koa tree, native to the Big Island of Hawaii, produces lumber in a variety of colors and hues, from light, honey yellow to dark, chocolate brown. This is a perfect project for all those pieces of wood that are too small or too irregular to use for anything large.

The larger shell box measures 1½" x 2" x 4". The larger leaf box is 1½" x 1¾" x 4¼". Each is made from a single block of wood.

• Using a band saw with a narrow, fine tooth blade, first rough-out the box shape in a block of koa or other figured wood. Slice off the lid, about ⁵⁄₁₆" thick. The finished lid will overhang the box by about ¼", so band saw the box body to reduce its size. Then slice off the bottom, about ³⁄₁₆" thick, and remove the center oval to create the hollow interior of the box. Glue the box back together with its bottom. Finish-sand the exterior surfaces of the box.

• Carve, shape, and finish-sand the top and the edges of the lid.

• To make the lid liner, mill a ³⁄₁₆"-thick block the shape of the interior of the box body. Fit it to the body; finish-sand its edges and one face, and glue it to the underside of the lid. Apply a hand-rubbed oil finish; wax and buff to a high luster.

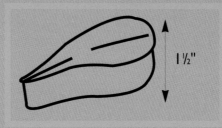

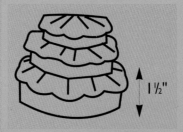

Gary White

Although Gary got his first woodwork training as a boy in his father's shop, he wasn't able to make woodworking a full time occupation until his retirement from the U.S. Air Force, where he attained the rank of Lieutenant Colonel. "For a time, during my years as a pilot flying C-130 transport aircraft, I was stationed in the Phillipines. Watching the local woodworkers there really inspired me. They are incredibly skilled at any wood-working technique you can think of, and they do everything by hand.

"After I retired, we bought a house in Oklahoma, and I put in a studio. To help with the payments, I began making furniture. But furniture is hard to make, and harder to sell, so my wife Jackie, who is a quilter, suggested I try making quilts

out of wood. I started doing wall hangings, but after a while, I wanted something that would be more of a challenge to me. Boxes have enabled me to incorporate what I learned about marquetry and design from the wall pieces. I've gotten a lot of support and encouragement from the Arkansas Craft Guild, which I joined in 1983, and that's helped me take my work farther."

Rather than cutting pieces for his marquetry designs out of thin veneers, Gary uses a band saw to mill ⅛"-thick slices from solid blocks. "I made quite a study of traditional American quilts," Gary says, "and most of the patterns I use are based on triangles and diamonds. I've found that out of hundreds of designs, people particularly like the ones with star shapes, so that's what I've concentrated on."

Quilt Pattern Boxes

Photo on page 40. Exploded diagram on page 43.

The lids of these colorful boxes have a marquetry inlay of geometric shapes based on American quilt designs. The hinged lid box is made of curly birch, a tree grown in Arkansas. The lid frame and slipfeathers are walnut. The marquetry pattern, called "Ohio Stars," is made of wenge, narra, soft maple, and curly birch.

• To make the hinged lid box, miter the four sides, following instructions for The Miter Joint on page 12. With a band saw, mill the thumb opening in the front of the box.
• Finish-sand the inside surfaces, and glue-up the box with the bottom in place. When the box is dry, make slots for the slipfeathers. Following the

instructions on page 13, mill the slipfeathers and glue them in place.

• Slice ⅛"-thick sections from solid blocks of wood using the band saw. An alternative is to use sheets of hardwood veneer, available in a wide variety of species from many lumber suppliers. Veneers with paper or cloth backing are easier to work with. Cut the parts for the design using a sharp utility knife or surgical scalpel, and apply to the ⅛"-plywood lid panel using spray or contact adhesive. Veneer is thin, so when finish sanding, be careful not to sand through it.

• Mill and miter the lid rails. These have a saw kerf dado, in which the edges of lid panel will sit. To allow for a precise fit of the finished lid, make it a hair larger than the box opening. After assembly, sand edges carefully as needed to fit. Assemble the lid, and when dry, mill the slipfeather slots in the corners. Glue in the slipfeathers.

• To install the lid, put it in the final position, jammed in place by means of thin strips of newspaper. Following instructions for Invisible Hinge Pins on page 15, use a drill press to drill holes for two hinge pins. These should be marked so that the pin will be in the vertical center of the edge of the lid, and far enough in from its rear edge so that when open, the lid stops at a comfortable angle. Maintain a gap of at least ¹⁄₁₆" between the rear the edge of the lid and the box side to allow for swing, and round-over the top of that edge.

• Once the lid has been fitted and pinned, remove it and carve the fingernail slot on the front edge. Finish-sand all the exterior surfaces of the box body, and glue in the lid support. Install the lid, countersinking hinge pins below the surface of the box, and then filling the holes with short lengths of matching wood dowel. Apply a hand-rubbed oil finish; wax and buff.

Quilt Pattern Box Lid close-up

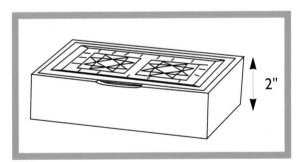

2"

Part	Description	Dimensions	Qty
A	Box front/back	$\frac{1}{4}$" x 2" x 8"	2
B	Box side	$\frac{1}{4}$" x 2" x 5$\frac{1}{4}$"	2
C	Bottom	$\frac{1}{8}$" x 4$\frac{7}{8}$" x 7$\frac{5}{8}$"	1
D	Lid support	$\frac{1}{4}$" x 1$\frac{1}{4}$" x 7$\frac{1}{2}$"	1
E	Lid rail	$\frac{1}{2}$" x $\frac{5}{8}$" x 7$\frac{3}{8}$"	2
F	Lid rail	$\frac{1}{2}$" x $\frac{5}{8}$" x 4$\frac{5}{8}$"	2
G	Lid marquetry panel	$\frac{1}{4}$" x 4$\frac{1}{8}$" x 6$\frac{7}{8}$"	1
H	Slipfeather	$\frac{1}{8}$" x $\frac{1}{2}$" x $\frac{1}{2}$"	12
J	Hinge pin	$\frac{1}{16}$" x $\frac{1}{2}$"	2

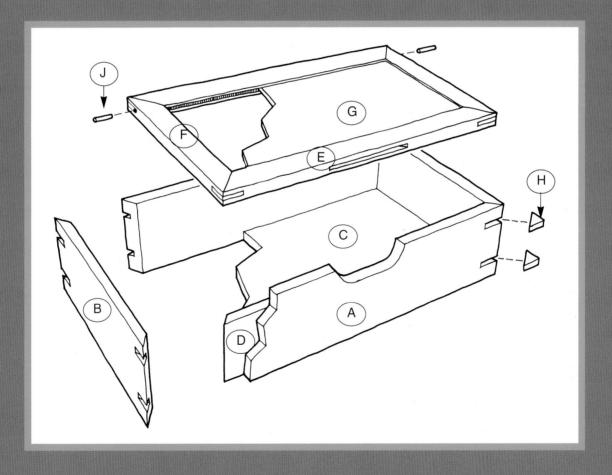

Patrick Leonard

Photo by Patrick Leonard

"Work smarter, not harder" has always been Patrick Leonard's motto. Like all woodworkers, however, he faces a familiar dilemma: how to meet the economic needs of his Pennsylvania-based business and family, without losing the sheer enjoyment and personal fulfillment of making beautiful things.

"When I was twelve, my mom and I put a workshop in the back of the trailer we were living in," Patrick remembers. "My only tools then were a Sears circular saw and a hammer, but I made a pine 5-drawer nightstand as a gift for my aunt. She still brags that she owns the very first piece of furniture I ever made." Over the years, Patrick developed his skills, and went on to make furniture of all types, including dressers, bedroom suites, scrollwork balusters for porches, coffee and dining tables, and chairs. "I've always wanted to learn everything there was to learn," Patrick says, "even though I know there's always something more."

Although he loves making furniture, the amount of time and effort required to market it proved an increasing drain. His desire to broaden his horizons led Patrick to begin making boxes. "Given my background, it's no surprise that my boxes incorporate furniture elements. Many of them are basically scaled-down versions of my furniture pieces, and I make them in limited editions. I can't wait to do more one-of-a-kind work, though. I've got sketches and drawings for a dozen new ideas."

Portable Cigar Box

Photo on page 44. Exploded diagram on page 47.

This practical seven-cigar maple carrying case has a simple but elegant lacewood sliding lid. Make the body of the box from a block of maple or any figured hardwood. Drill seven 1" diameter holes completely through the block. The box has a small stripe detail, not shown in the drawing, that runs along either edge.

• Mill a $\frac{1}{4}$" dado $\frac{1}{16}$" deep, and glue in the edge strips (Part F).
• Mill the stock for the top (Part B). On the underside of the top, mill a dado, $1\frac{3}{8}$" wide and $\frac{1}{16}$" deep, centered on the long axis of the part, and running almost its entire length. This will accommodate the sliding lid. Finish the end of the dado with a chisel as needed, and then glue

on the top and the bottom, being careful not to allow glue to clog the top dado.

• When the glue is dry, use a router with a $1\frac{1}{4}$"-diameter bit to remove the long central area of the top, leaving a radius at end. Then switch to a round-over bit, and use the router to radius the sides of the box. Drill and install the ball catch.

• The sliding lid can be rabbeted on the table saw to produce the $\frac{1}{16}$"-thick flange that glides

> Natural wood is a marvellous material, and much of the appeal of a wooden box comes from the maker's skill in revealing the wood's inherent beauty. This is a powerful argument for keeping designs as simple as possible.
> —T.L.

Portable Cigar Box open

in the slot on the top. Use the drill press to mill the shallow depression on the outer surface of the lid, as well as the groove on the underside of the lid, which gives the tips of the cigars additional clearance as the lid slides shut. Adjust the fit of the sliding lid, and finish-sand.

Note: Patrick uses a durable, environmentally safe water-based finish on all his boxes.

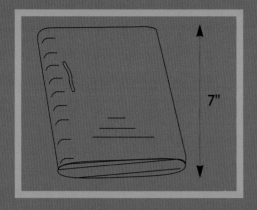

7"

Part	Description	Dimensions	Qty
A	Box body	$1\frac{1}{2}$" x 7" x 7"	1
B	Top	$\frac{1}{4}$" x $1\frac{1}{2}$" x 7"	1
C	Lid	$\frac{1}{4}$" x $1\frac{1}{4}$" x $6\frac{3}{4}$"	1
D	Ball catch	$\frac{1}{8}$" diameter	1
E	Bottom	$\frac{1}{4}$" x $1\frac{1}{2}$" x 7"	1
F	Edge strip*	$\frac{1}{16}$" x $\frac{1}{4}$" x 7"	2

*not shown

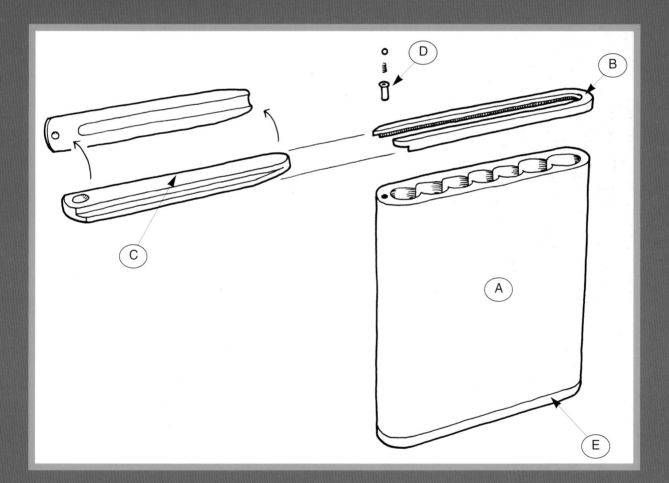

Gregory Williams

It was in 1974, while living near Bear Wallow, Kentucky, that Greg Williams realized he had a greater affinity for woodworking than for the chemical engineering he had been studying in school. Not long afterward, an elderly blues guitar player agreed to sell Greg a set of woodworking tools, and that settled the matter.

Greg named his woodworking business "Zeke Towne Woodworks" after an historic Kentuckian. A short series of visits to New York City during the 1980's had the greatest impact on the distinctive shapes of his boxes. "I took a night school course in design that led me to books on Mayan architecture and Art Deco. After I came back home, any chunk of wood I picked up to work on just seemed to go that Mayan Deco way.

"Not long afterward, an old pallet factory in my neighborhood closed down. One thing led to another, and I ended up owning thousands of board feet of lumber, all native Appalachian species like butternut, hickory, walnut, and cherry. Anymore, I don't go to the lumberyard. I am the lumberyard." Thanks to his engineering background, Greg has an uncanny ability to combine these woods into unusual constructions and elaborate shapes.

Business Card Box

Photo on page 48. Exploded diagram on page 50.

This flip-top box for business cards, a marvel of compactness and ingenuity, is made from a single block of wood. Making it requires careful milling, so it is advisable to experiment with the design using scrap wood before making a final version.

• To create the final version, select a piece of highly figured wood (spalted maple was used in the example shown) about $\frac{3}{4}$" x $3\frac{1}{8}$" x 5". Using a table saw or band saw with a fine-toothed blade, slice off the two sides (Part C). With a band saw, carefully separate the bottom (Part B) from card receptacle (Part A).
• Using the band saw, separate the exterior portion of the top from the interior portion, into which the cards will eventually fit. Band saw off the upper $\frac{1}{4}$" thickness of the top. Use a dado blade on the table saw to mill a

Business Card Box closed

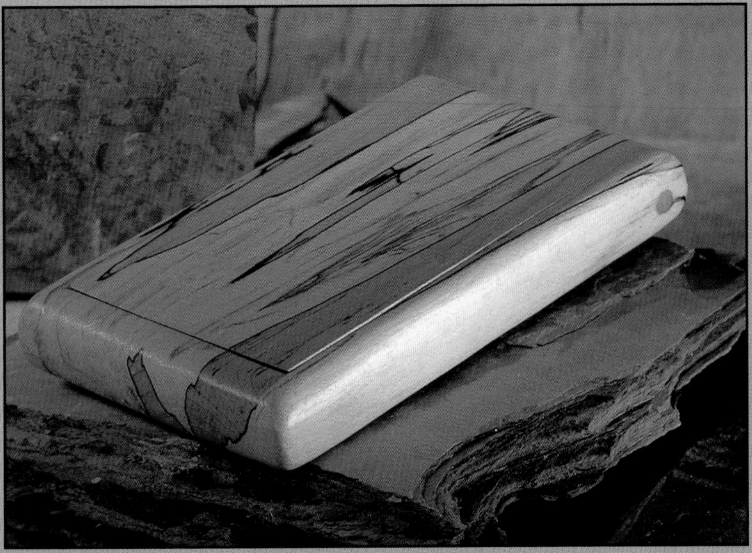

2" wide by ¼"-deep dado in the interior portion, then glue the interior and exterior portions back together. Sand the interior surfaces of the bottom (Part B) and the sides (Part C) and use the drill press to drill 3/16"-diameter holes to receive the hinge pins.

• Make a trial assembly using masking tape to ensure that all parts fit snugly, then glue the box. Finish-sand, oil, wax, and polish.

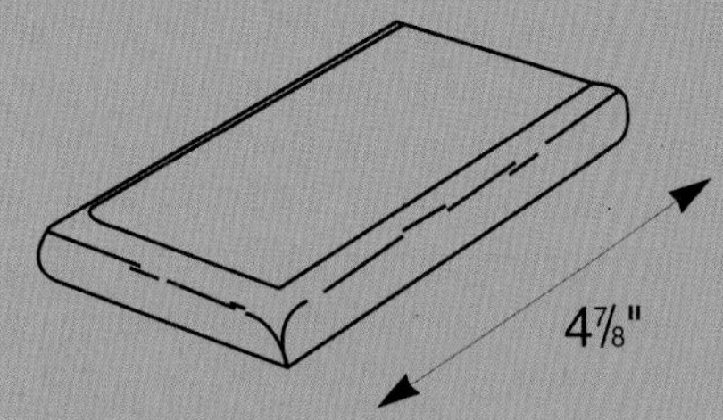

Part	Description	Dimensions	Qty
A	Top/card receptacle	¾" x 2½" x 4½"	1
B	Bottom	¾" x 2½" x 2⅝"	1
C	Side	¼" x ¾" x 4⅞"	2
D	Hinge pin	3/16" x ½"	2

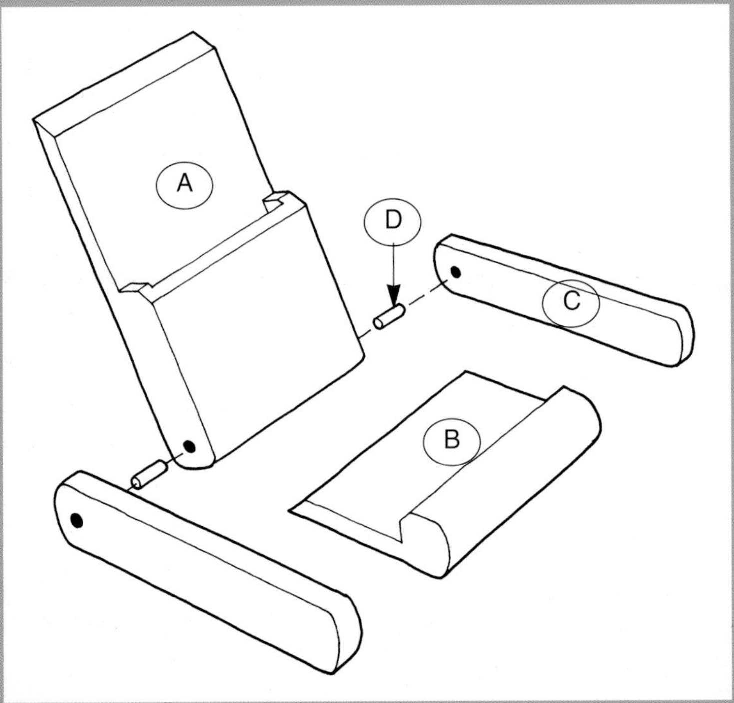

Oval Boxes

Exploded diagram on page 52.

These boxes can be made in a wide variety of sizes, proportions, and woods. The body and lid of each box are band sawed from a single block of wood. In the example shown, this block is made up of three separate pieces of wood laminated together. Because of the difficulty of working with short lengths, plan to make this box in a batch of three or more.

• To make a batch of three boxes, start by preparing the laminate block. Mill a 10"-long strip of oak or other light wood, 2⅛" x 1¼". Mill two 10"-long strips of walnut or other contrasting dark wood, each 1" x 2⅛".

Following the instructions for Laminates on page 15, glue-up the three strips to produce a final laminated block whose dimensions are 2⅛" x 3¼" x 10".

• Crosscut the block into three pieces 2¾" long. Each piece will become a box. Using the band saw, slice off the two ¼"-thick sides (Part C) and the lid (Part B). Using masking tape, reassemble the box to mark and drill ³⁄₁₆"-diameter holes for the hinge pins. Finish-sand the interior surfaces, then assemble with lid and hinge pins in place. Use a 1"-diameter sanding sleeve on the drill press to mill the thumb slot in the front of the box body.

• Finish-shape and sand the entire box on the 6" x 48" belt sander, then apply a spray varnish or lacquer.

Oval Box open

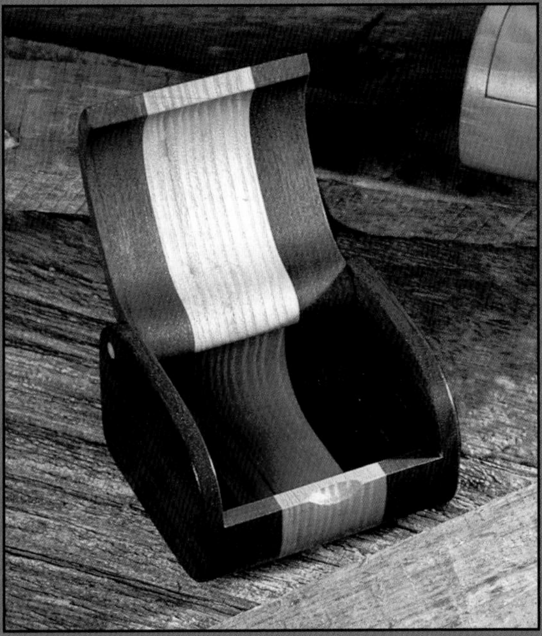

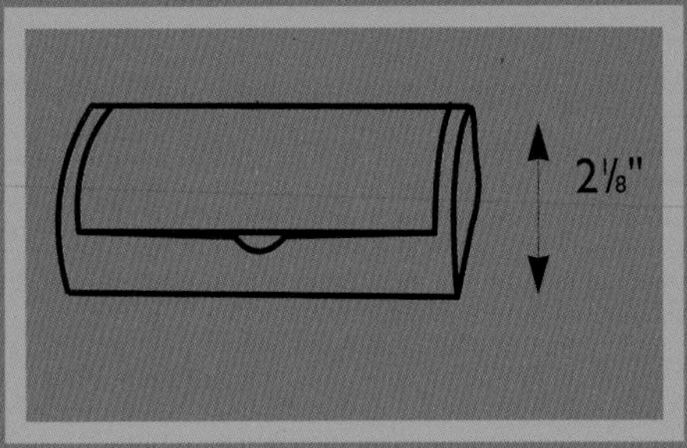

Part	Description	Dimensions	Qty
A	Box body block size	2⅛" x 2¹¹⁄₁₆" x 3¼"	1
B	Lid block size	2⅛" x 2¹¹⁄₁₆" x 3¼"	1
C	Side	¼" x 2⅛" x 2¾"	2
D	Hinge pin	³⁄₁₆" x ½"	2

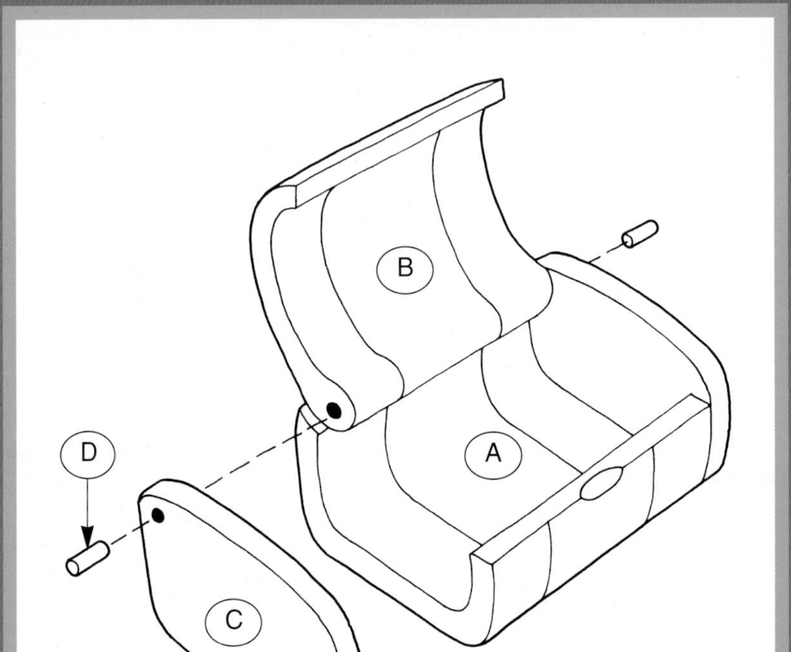

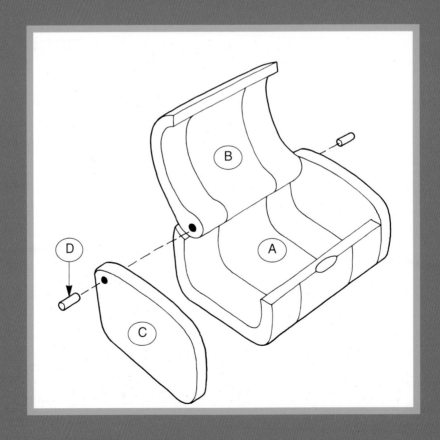

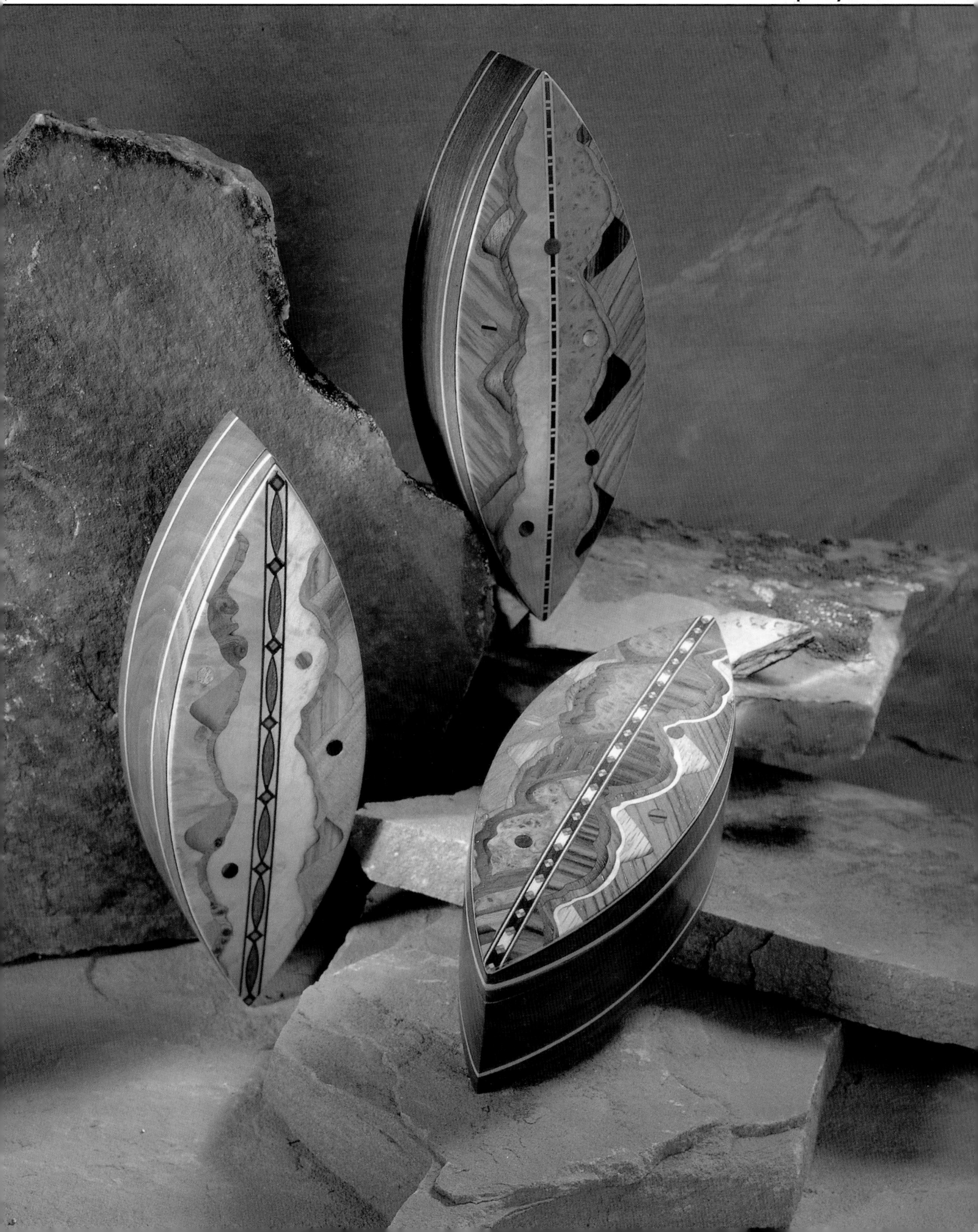

T. Breeze VerDant

Photo by Robin Rieske

Although he has long been a master of conventional marquetry, with its floral motifs and repeated geometric designs, T. Breeze VerDant's latest work takes the technique into new territories of abstraction. Some of the geometric elements remain, but the fluid shapes and fascinating color combinations he is currently producing in his Vermont studio suggest imaginary, almost psychological landscapes.

"I have a long history with trees," Breeze remembers. "As a child, I could always be found up in them. As an adult, I logged them to build myself a log cabin, and to produce enough firewood to see me through the long Adirondack winters. I never cease to be awed by trees, by their inward and outward beauty, and am respectful of the essential role they play in all aspects of our life.

"I've been a student in many different settings," says Breeze, "including the school of hard knocks, from which making these boxes should earn me a doctoral degree. Marquetry allows me to be creative with wood; I get to work with the natural enchantment of so many different species. I like the fact that while my work celebrates trees, it has a minimal impact on them. I use native hardwoods like poplar, sycamore, cherry, holly, and maple, and scrap and cutoffs whenever I can.

"Marquetry is an ancient craft, one that combines the natural and the artistic in a way I like. With it, I feel I've found a chance to achieve my goal: to stun people with the beauty of wood grain, and be happy doing it."

Marquetry Boxes

Photo on page 53. Exploded diagram on page 56.

This box begins as a single block of walnut, 2¼" x 2½" x 6½". The veneers in the marquetry design on the surface of the lid include amboyna, aspen, narra, padouk, satinwood, lemonwood, bubinga, red gum, koto, kingwood, cocobolo, maple, tulipwood, redwood burl, ebony, and rosewood. The stripe down the center of each lid is a section of guitar purfling, a specialized product available from musical instrument suppliers in a wide variety of designs.

• Using a band saw, rough-cut the pointed oval or canoe shape. Band saw off the upper portion of the lid (Part D) ⁷⁄₁₆" thick, and the box bottom (Part C) ¼" thick. (After the bottom liner is installed, this will be glued back on.)

• Use the band saw to remove the center section of the box body, creating the hollow interior of the box. Slice a ⅛"-thick section off the upper edge of the box; this will become the lower portion of the lid (Part G).

• The thin double veneers of maple plus lacewood or koa that produce the lid liner and the bottom liner (Part B and Part F) are visible on the outside of the box as decorative horizontal bands. Since their edges show, use solid wood veneers, rather than veneers with a backing of softwood, cloth or paper. The maple veneer, whose edges produce the horizontal white band, is 1/16" thick. Glued to it

is a 1/64"-thick veneer, either lacewood (top) or koa (bottom). When box and lid are glued up, these parts are sandwiched between the lid and lid liner, and between the box body and bottom.

• Use a surgical scalpel or sharp utility knife to cut the veneer. Irregular shapes can be perfectly matched by stacking veneers, then cutting through several sheets at a time. Breeze has peppered his abstract designs with ¼" discs of contrasting woods.

• Use a file to round-over the tips of the brass alignment pins, and install two at one end of the box, and one at the other, to ensure that the top will fit perfectly. Finish-sand the entire box, and apply a coat of spray lacquer inside and out.

Marquetry Boxes open

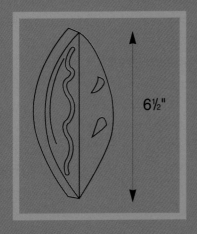

6½"

Part	Description	Dimensions	Qty
A	Box body	1" x 2⅜" x 6½"	1
B	Double veneer layer/bottom liner	5/64" x 2⅜" x 6½"	1
C	Box bottom	¼" x 2⅜" x 6½"	1
D	Lid	7/16" x 2⅜" x 6½"	1
E	Marquetry	1/16" x 2⅜" x 6½"	
F	Double veneer layer/lid liner	5/64" x 2⅜" x 6½"	1
G	Lid rim	⅛" x 2⅜" x 6½"	1
H	Brass alignment pin	⅛" x ½"	3

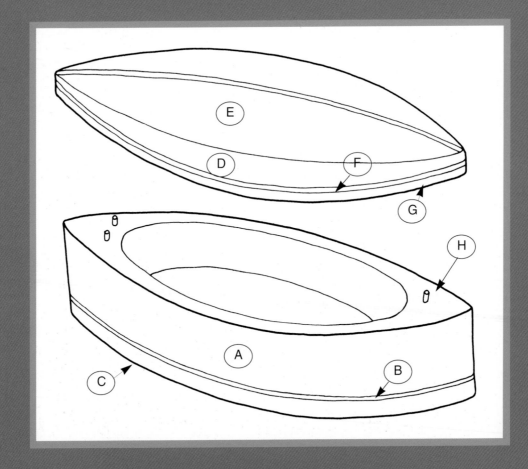

Bradford Rockwell

"Today, people call me 'The Box Man,'" writes Bradford Rockwell from his New England studio, "but I didn't start out making boxes—in fact, I've never taken any woodworking courses. I went to art school in Boston to study illustration and cartooning. I guess I must have been interested in boxes even then, because I notice that in some of my old cartoons, instead of drawing balloons around the words my characters spoke, I used little expanding boxes.

"After art school, I found myself living in a friend's woodshop, working for him one day a week in exchange for rent. I started out making boxes to hold cigarettes, but very quickly realized that these appealed to only a limited market. So I changed the design, and came up with my box for credit cards or business cards."

After working for a time as a carpenter's helper, Brad was able to equip a shop of his own, where in addition to boxes he has made wood briefcases, mirror stands, and cover plates for electrical outlets. "I always think the world is a big old cartoon," Brad says, "and I like the surrealistic side of things. One day for no particular reason I made a set of four small nesting boxes. People loved them, and wanted to buy them. So just to see how far I could go, I made another set, even smaller, with six boxes, and finally my famous set of eight, which belongs to a collector in Walpole, New Hampshire."

Credit Card Box

Photo on page 57. Exploded diagram on page 59.

This box for credit cards or business cards can be made in an infinite combination of solid or laminated woods. The example shown is birdseye maple, with a lid laminated of maple, walnut, ebony, and African vermilion.

Credit Card Box open

• Mill the box sides, bottom, front and back. For strength, a modified tenon on the ends of the sides (Part A) fits into a corresponding slot in the back. The inside face of each side is also slotted to accept the rabbeted edge of the lid. These slots can be milled with a router, or on the table saw.

• Finish-sand the interior surfaces and assemble the box body. To make the laminated lid, follow the instructions for Laminates on page 15. To ensure a strong connection between the lid and the lid rail (Part F), mill a dado on the inside face of the lid rail (not shown in the diagram), and insert the edge of the lid into it when gluing. Check for fit and adjust as necessary.

• Finish-sand all exterior surfaces. Apply a hand-rubbed oil finish; wax and buff.

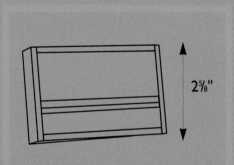

2⅝"

Part	Description	Dimensions	Qty
A	Side	$^{3}/_{16}$" x $^{3}/_{4}$" x $3^{15}/_{16}$"	2
B	Front	$^{3}/_{16}$" x $^{1}/_{2}$" x $2^{5}/_{8}$"	1
C	Back	$^{3}/_{16}$" x $^{3}/_{4}$" x $2^{5}/_{8}$"	1
D	Bottom	$^{1}/_{8}$" x $2^{3}/_{16}$" x $3^{13}/_{16}$"	1
E	Lid	$^{3}/_{16}$" x $2^{1}/_{4}$" x $3^{7}/_{8}$"	1
F	Lid rail	$^{3}/_{16}$" x $^{1}/_{4}$" x $2^{5}/_{8}$"	1

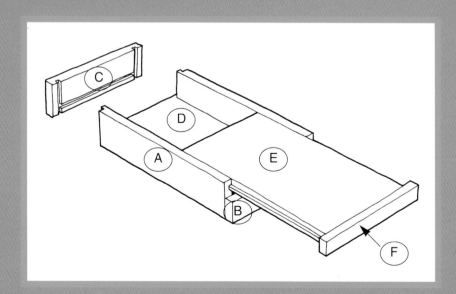

Inch Box Set

See photo on page 60. See Credit Card Box
exploded diagram on page 59.

It is difficult to believe that this extraordinary set of
eight nesting boxes, which seems to represent the ultimate
in miniaturization, could actually have been built by human
hand and eye. When asked how he makes something so
small, Brad's first reply is, "Carefully!"

The eight box, bubinga and bocote, set ranges in size
from a 1" cube, with walls $\frac{1}{16}$" thick, to a $\frac{1}{8}$" cube, with
walls $\frac{1}{32}$" thick. Each box has an operable lid. The
dimensions listed are for the largest box in the set, and the
basic design is similar to Brad's Credit Card Box exploded
diagram on page 59, except that in this smaller version, the
side walls are joined by a simple butt joint. The lids slide in

> In addition to the
> satisfaction of a job well
> done, making an original
> box provides the sheer
> excitement of seeing your
> own vision made real. Out
> of the multitude of life's
> unrealized possibilities, here
> is one idea that somehow
> has made its way into
> concrete form. Suddenly
> there it is on your
> workbench: something of
> you proclaiming, *I made this,*
> *this is me.*
>
> —T.L.

Inch Box Set open

a narrow dado, and in all but the tiniest three boxes, each lid has a front rail for easy opening.

• Start by making the smallest box in the set, and work up to the largest. Each box is made from a four-sided tube, then crosscut to final size. To make handling the material easier, these tubes can be much longer than needed.
• Mill enough $1/16$"-thick stock to make eight tubes of increasing size. To simplify the process of milling dados, make stock wide enough so that it can be ripped lengthwise to yield all four sides of each tube. Using a thin-kerf saw blade, mill two shallow dados on the inside face of the stock, parallel to the grain and $1/16$" in from the edge. Then rip the stock to produce the four sides of the tube.

Note: The key to successful handling of material this small is to wrap the tube in masking tape to hold parts in place while gluing. Similar masking tape wrapping will protect the tubes from being blown away or chipped while crosscutting.

• Glue-up the tube for the smallest box, making certain the sides with dados are opposite each other. Glue the bottom on to one end the of tube. Make a jig on the table saw miter fence that will hold both the wrapped tube and the cut off box securely in place, and crosscut the box to final size. Then, with the box stuck to the workbench on two-sided tape, use a small utility knife to remove a section from the top of one side, to allow the lid to clear the side when opened. Fabricate and install the sliding lid.
• Follow the same procedure for the next larger box.

Note: The lids of the three smallest boxes do not have a front rail. Brad makes each successively larger box a hair too small to allow the next smaller box to fit inside it. He then sands the six exterior faces of the smaller box until it fits perfectly. This is why the stock for the smallest boxes starts out $1/16$" thick, and ends up (after sanding) about $1/32$" thick.

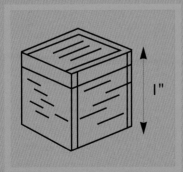

Part	Description	Dimensions	Qty
A	Side	$1/16$" x 1" x 1"	2
B	Side	$1/16$" x 1" x $7/8$"	2
C	Bottom	$1/16$" x $7/8$" x $7/8$"	1
D	Lid	$1/16$" x $15/16$" x $15/16$"	1
E	Lid rail	$1/16$" x $1/16$" x 1"	1

Timothy Lydgate

Photo by T. Lydgate

Timothy Lydgate's earliest memories are of the frosty New England woods, where his father and elder brothers chopped and split cord after cord of oak, hickory, and cherry firewood for their living room fireplace. Warmly bundled against the cold, he was lulled to sleep by the rhythmic swish of the two-man saw, and when the crack of splitting logs awakened him, his toys were often fragrant chunks of fresh-cut hardwood.

After Timothy's formal education, he explored Europe, Africa, and Asia, absorbing diverse cultural and artistic traditions. He began woodworking after returning to his family's roots in the South Pacific in the 1970's. "In the Islands, I rediscovered the pleasure of wood. I came under the spell of iliahi, kou, kamani, ohia, and the other native tropical species, especially the highly figured ones, and that started me on what's becoming a lifelong search for the perfect burled, birdseye, or curly log."

Many of Timothy's boxes feature lids with what appears to be a marquetry design. These designs are actually made from solid wood laminates, rather than thin veneers, and are laboriously assembled, milled, and re-milled to create their complex and intricate patterns.

Inlaid Boxes

Photo on page 63. Exploded diagram on page 66.

These box designs lend themselves to endless variations in size, proportions, and wood combinations. Those shown in the photograph are made from African vermilion, East Indian rosewood, and white sapwood Hawaiian koa. (Like many species of hardwood, koa logs occasionally contain an area of light-colored wood just beneath the bark).

• To make the hinge-lid box at left in the photographs, start by fabricating the four sides, following the instructions for Laminates on page 15. Prepare a $\frac{1}{4}$"-thick laminate, $1\frac{5}{8}$" wide and about 13" long, of African vermilion, sapwood koa (or other light colored, contrasting wood) and East Indian rosewood. Crosscut and miter.
• Mill the bottom, finish-sand the interior surfaces, and glue up the box. When dry, use a jig to mill slots for slipfeathers, and glue slipfeathers in place.

• The lid is made by mitering four 2½"-long sections of a laminate rail, 1" in width, and 5/16" thick, made of the same African vermilion, rosewood, and white koa. Like the four sides of a picture frame, these mitered parts produce a perfect square. In the center of the square, Timothy inserts four thin pieces of Indian rosewood, their axes slightly offset to enliven the visual interest of the design.

• Following the instructions for Invisible Hinge Pins on page 15, jam fit the lid in place, and drill holes for the hinge pins. Finish-sand the edges and interior surfaces, and round-over the upper portion of the back edge. Install the lid and hinge pins. Countersink the ends of the hinge pins, and cover them with plugs (not shown in the diagram) made from 1/16" diameter vermilion dowels. No thumb slot is needed; these boxes are opened by applying gentle pressure to the rear edge of the lid.

• Finish-sand the exterior surfaces, oil, wax, and buff. Line the bottom with midnight blue ultrasuede.

Inlaid Boxes open

65

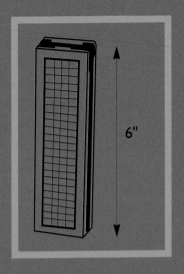

6"

Part	Description	Dimensions	Qty
A	Side	$\frac{1}{4}$" x $1\frac{5}{8}$" x $3\frac{1}{16}$"	4
B	Bottom	$\frac{1}{8}$" x $2\frac{1}{2}$" x $2\frac{1}{2}$"	1
C	Lid	$\frac{5}{16}$" x $2\frac{1}{2}$" x $2\frac{1}{2}$"	1
D	Hinge pin	$\frac{1}{16}$" x $\frac{1}{2}$"	2
E	Slipfeather	$\frac{1}{8}$" x $\frac{1}{2}$" x $\frac{1}{2}$"	16
F	Lid support *	$\frac{1}{8}$" x $\frac{1}{4}$" x $2\frac{9}{16}$"	1

*(not drawn)

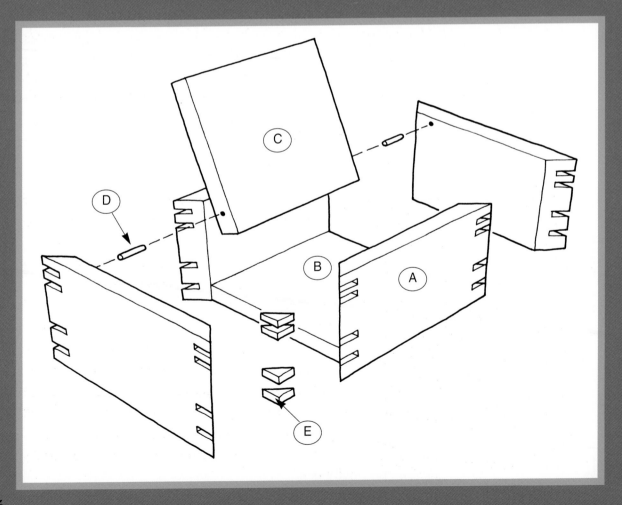

Ed Love

Photo by Alfred Batungbacal

"I got started in woodworking out of necessity," says Ed Love. "I love being around the water, so it seemed natural for me to join the Coast Guard. The headquarters building where I was first stationed was pretty bare, and I needed furniture. After that, woodworking just kind of evolved into a hobby. People liked what I made, and more and more of them wanted to buy it."

During his service with the Coast Guard, Ed went to flight school and became a helicopter pilot. "I started my first buckle box about four years ago, when I was on reserve duty," Ed remembers. "But then I got called back to active duty, so I had to put it on the shelf. Someday soon I hope to be able to do woodworking full time.

"I was a ceramics major in college, and I have a good sense of design. What I like about woodworking is that it's creative, and you have to use your head a lot. I'd been making stacking boxes for a while, but I'm always searching for new twists, and that's when I got the idea for the buckle boxes. I have fun trying to make things appear what they aren't—sort of like a joke on the eyes."

Koa and Ebony Buckle Chests

Photo on page 67. Exploded diagram on page 69.

This stacking box of highly figured curly Hawaiian koa, with ebony "straps" and brass buckles, is glued up as a single rectangular solid, then crosscut on the table saw to produce the three sections. To allow for saw cuts and sanding, the original solid should be 4" tall.

• Miter the four sides, and mill saw kerf dados for the two bottoms. Glue-up the box with the two bottoms and lid top panel (Part F) in place.
• When the box is dry, use a ½"-dado blade on the table saw to mill shallow dados on the outside of two sides and top, into which pieces of ebony that mimic leather straps will be glued. Carve the ebony for the top of the lid (Part G) to look like strap ends. Remove

the straight base side of the two brass buckles, and size the buckles to fit the carved straps. Finish-sand the outside surfaces of box, and the ebony parts, and then glue them in place in the dados.
• Following the instructions on page 14, slice the box into three sections. Highly figured wood is prone to chipping and tear-out; this can be prevented by wrapping the area to be cut with masking tape, and using a sharp carbide saw blade. Sand the edges of the cuts, and mill and install the upper and lower liners, which can be made of maple or any available light-colored wood.
• Apply a hand-rubbed oil finish; wax, and buff. Using a small quantity of epoxy, glue the brass buckles in place.
• Following the instructions for Velvet Linings on page 13, line the two bottoms with velvet pads.

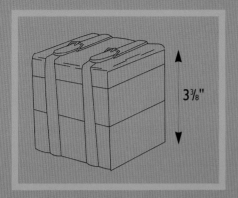

Part	Description	Dimensions	Qty
A	Lower side	$\frac{1}{4}$" x $1\frac{1}{2}$" x $3\frac{7}{16}$"	4
B	Middle side	$\frac{1}{4}$" x $1\frac{5}{16}$" x $3\frac{7}{16}$"	4
C	Lid side	$\frac{1}{4}$" x $\frac{9}{16}$" x $3\frac{7}{16}$"	4
D	Bottom	$\frac{1}{8}$" x $3\frac{1}{8}$" x $3\frac{1}{8}$"	1
E	Bottom	$\frac{1}{8}$" x $3\frac{1}{8}$" x $3\frac{1}{8}$"	1
F	Lid top panel	$\frac{1}{4}$" x $3\frac{7}{16}$" x $3\frac{7}{16}$"	1
G	Ebony detailing	$\frac{1}{4}$" x $\frac{1}{2}$" x $3\frac{3}{4}$"	2
H	Brass buckle	as req'd	2
J	Ebony detailing	$\frac{1}{8}$" x $\frac{1}{2}$" x $3\frac{3}{4}$"	4
K	Upper liner	$\frac{3}{16}$" x $\frac{7}{8}$" x $2\frac{15}{16}$"	4
L	Lower liner	$\frac{3}{16}$" x $\frac{15}{16}$" x $2\frac{15}{16}$"	4

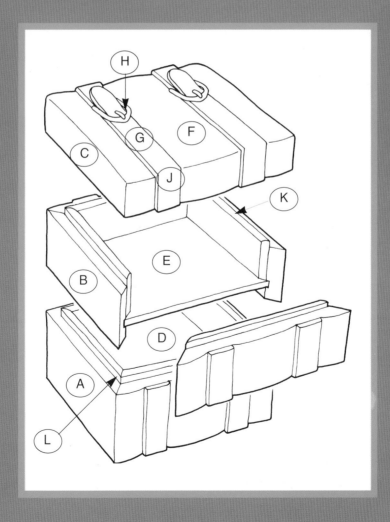

Ray Jones

Photo by Tim Barnwell

Ray Jones received his first exposure to woodwork as a carpenter's helper during summers while in college. He received his degree in aeronautical engineering, and moved to Southern California to work for an aerospace propulsion firm.

While setting up his first household, he bought tools instead of furniture, and then used them to build the furniture. "I'm intrigued by the tremendous variety of woods that exist in the world," says Ray. "Once I got my home finished, I turned my woodworking attention to making gifts, including a jewelry box for my future wife. It wasn't long before I left my engineering job, and began woodworking full time.

"I believe that a wood box should be just that—wood. As much as possible, I use only wood in my boxes, including the fasteners, hinges, and drawer slides. I'm fascinated by wooden mechanisms, and the intersections of various geometric shapes. I try to use environmentally friendly species of lumber, including rarely seen West Coast varieties, lesser known species from planned forestry projects in South America, and recently some tropical exotics salvaged from the Florida Keys."

Chest of Drawers

Photo on page 70. Exploded diagram on page 72.

This prototype miniature chest of drawers is a marvel of engineering. It consists of a shell of madrone burl, into which are glued differently sized drawer platforms of Baltic birch plywood. (Dimensions given are for the largest drawer.)

• To make the shell, start by lathe turning a shallow, flat-rimmed bowl 6" in diameter. Cut the bowl in half, and reglue edge to edge, laminating a $\frac{1}{4}$"-wide strip of contrasting wood between the two parts.

• Use a router to hollow the drawer bodies out of a $\frac{7}{8}$" thickness of Baltic birch plywood. These are attached to solid walnut drawer fronts. The drawer fronts are glued up as one block, with a single piece of $\frac{1}{8}$" plywood glued vertically along the midline in a saw kerf dado. This walnut block is then sliced to final dimension. The resulting sections of the $\frac{1}{8}$" plywood strip serve as drawer handles. A dovetailed rail glued to the bottom of the drawers runs in a matching slot in each drawer platform. Following the instructions for Velvet Linings on page 13, line each drawer with a velvet pad.

Chest of Drawers open

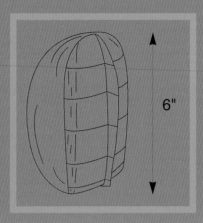

6"

Part	Description	Dimensions	Qty
A	Shell	$\frac{1}{4}$" x $3\frac{3}{8}$" x 6"	1
B	Drawer platform	$\frac{1}{4}$" x $2\frac{3}{4}$" x 3"	4
C	Base	$\frac{1}{4}$" x $2\frac{3}{4}$" x 3"	1
D	Drawer front	$\frac{7}{8}$" x $1\frac{1}{4}$" x $3\frac{1}{4}$"	5
E	Drawer bottom	$\frac{1}{8}$" x 2" x $2\frac{7}{8}$"	4
F	Drawer body	$\frac{7}{8}$" x $2\frac{1}{8}$" x $2\frac{3}{4}$"	4
G	Drawer rail	$\frac{1}{4}$" x $\frac{1}{2}$" x $2\frac{3}{4}$"	4
H	Handle	$\frac{1}{8}$" x $\frac{3}{4}$" x $1\frac{1}{4}$"	1

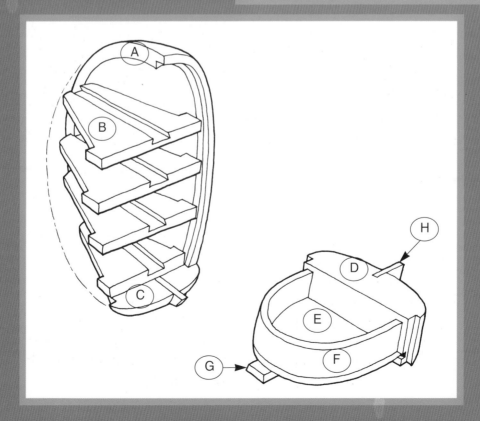

Baltic Birch Boxes

Exploded diagram page 74.

Like many of Ray Jones' designs, this intriguing box reflects its maker's training in both aerodynamics and engineering. It also shows off his fondness for highly figured woods, including spalted beech and curly myrtle. Although the design is ultimately simple, getting the hang of it requires time, so it is advisable to make a version or two using scrap wood before attempting the final piece.

• The body of the box consists of a ½" Baltic birch plywood base (Part E), attached to a rounded front and back. Glue these up, along with the compartment sides. Assemble the sides and the lid (Parts B and C), and then slice the sides diagonally. The forward section of each side is then glued and dowelled to the front (Part A).

• To attach the lid, first drill two $\frac{5}{16}$" diameter holes, and glue in two plugs made of contrasting woods (Part H). When these are dry and sanded flush, jam the lid in place with bits of newspaper, and drill a smaller diameter hole for the two dowels that serve as hinge pins (Part G).

• Install the lid, then shape and finish-sand the exterior of the box using a 6" x 48" belt sander with progressively finer grits. Apply a hand-rubbed oil finish; wax and buff. Following the instructions for Velvet Linings on page 13, line with a velvet pad.

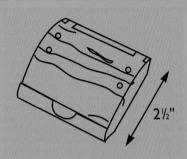

Part	Description	Dimensions	Qty
A	Front	$\frac{5}{8}$" x $\frac{7}{8}$" x $2\frac{3}{8}$"	1
B	Side	$\frac{1}{2}$" x $1\frac{1}{4}$" x $3\frac{3}{4}$"	2
C	Top	$\frac{1}{2}$" x $2\frac{7}{8}$" x 3"	1
D	Compartment side	$\frac{1}{8}$" x $\frac{3}{16}$" x $2\frac{1}{8}$"	2
E	Bottom	$\frac{1}{2}$" x $2\frac{3}{8}$" x $3\frac{5}{8}$"	1
F	Back	$\frac{5}{8}$" x $\frac{7}{8}$" x $2\frac{3}{8}$"	1
G	Dowel	$\frac{3}{16}$" x $\frac{3}{4}$"	6
H	Plug	$\frac{5}{16}$" x $\frac{1}{2}$"	

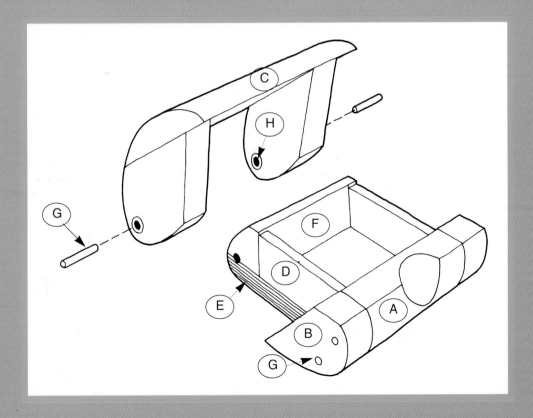

Terry Hufft

Photo by Brian Duffy

Terry Hufft worked for twenty-five years as a carpenter building new homes. "I'm very detail oriented," he says, "and in construction, a lot of the work is so far away from perfection that I found it aggravating. I'd been a carpenter since I got out of high school. One of the first projects I worked on was helping remodel my parents' restaurant. But construction just didn't offer enough of what I love, which is fine detail."

Besides detail, moving from carpentry to boxmaking has also given Terry the opportunity to focus on his interest in sculpture. "I like non-square, non-angular shapes, with curves and rounded edges. I think of my work as sculpture, and one reason why I chose to make boxes is because they're objects that have a potential use. They don't have to be used to be enjoyed.

"There's only so much you can do with the basic box, so for me, handles are the most creative part. I like to keep things simple, and emphasize the primitive, symmetrical aspects of my designs. I do a lot of sketching and playing around on paper, but everything I make is a series of unplanned accidents. I won't know how I'm going to sculpt a particular idea until I get it on the table saw."

Sculptural Boxes

Photo on page 75. Exploded Diagram on page 78.

The body and lid of this box are made of zebrawood; the splines and handle base are ebony, and the handle is lacewood.

• To make the body, mill the bottom (Part B), which rests on a rabbet, and mill and miter the four ⅞"-thick sides (Part A). Finish-sand the inside faces of the four sides and glue up the box. When dry, turn it upside down and mill four saw kerf dados for the splines (Part C). Before making these cuts, use a block of scrap wood to decide whether to leave the saw blade set at its customary 90 degree angle, or to change the angle slightly for visual effect. After milling, glue in the splines.
• Make the lid (Part D) from a solid block of wood, with the grain running vertically. A laminate of one or more woods can be used if wide enough stock is not available. Before beginning to shape the lid, use a table saw to mill a rabbet on underside of lid (this rabbet is not visible in the diagram). This will permit the lid to stay in place when set on the box.

• The body of the box can now be given its sloping, angled shape. Use a coarse grit belt on the 6" x 48" stationary belt sander to rough-out this shape, and do the same with the lid. Final-shape the lid and box together. Use tape or bits of newspaper to jam the lid in place, then change to a fine grit belt to complete the shaping process.

• Part G, the handle, fits in a saw kerf dado on Part F, the handle base. Mill Part F as a longer rail, and crosscut to final length after the dado is milled. Create its shape using the 6" x 48" belt sander. Rough-out the shape of the lacewood handle on the band saw, and finish on the belt sander. Drill holes for the attachment dowels, finish-sand, and assemble the lid and handle. When glue is dry, sand off any excess length of the attachment dowels that hold the handle to its base.

• Apply a hand-rubbed oil finish; wax and buff. Following the instructions for Velvet Linings on page 13, line box with velvet or ultrasuede. *Note: The dimensions and diagram on the next page refer to the zebrawood box at the right in the photographs. The box on the left is constructed in the same manner, except that the handle is a single piece of ebony, and the lid is a slightly more complex design.*

Sculptural Boxes open

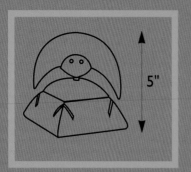

5"

Part	Description	Dimensions	Qty
A	Side	$\frac{7}{8}$" x $1\frac{1}{2}$" x $3\frac{7}{8}$"	4
B	Bottom	$\frac{1}{4}$" x $2\frac{3}{4}$" x $2\frac{3}{4}$"	1
C	Spline	$\frac{1}{8}$" x 1" x $1\frac{1}{2}$"	4
D	Lid	$\frac{13}{16}$" x $2\frac{1}{2}$" x $2\frac{1}{2}$"	1
E	Attachment dowel	$\frac{3}{16}$" x $\frac{1}{2}$"	3
F	Handle base	$\frac{5}{16}$" x 1" x $1\frac{1}{2}$"	1
G	Handle	$\frac{1}{8}$" x 3" x $4\frac{5}{8}$"	1

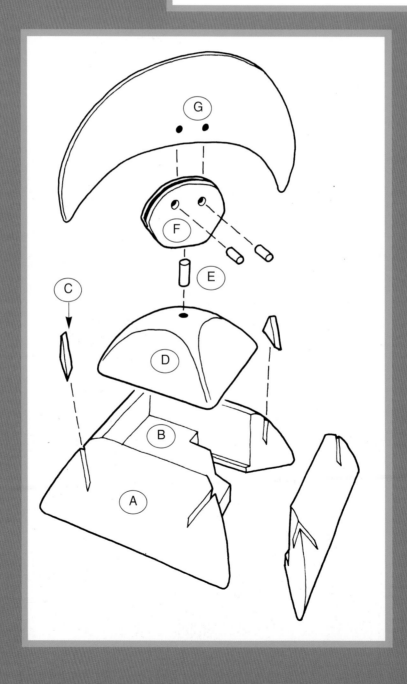

Coopered Chest

Katherine Heller

"When I was in high school I saw a wood carving that was so inspiring that I decided I wanted to learn how to make it. I started doing little stuff on my own, until I found a position as a sign carver's apprentice, where I learned to incise letters, flowers, and pictures. I was so intrigued by woodworking that while I was in college, I worked at woodworking every chance I got.

"After a while, though, carving pictures in wood lost its appeal. I started liking the wood better than the pictures. At this point I found another apprenticeship, this time with a furniture maker in Colorado. As luck would have it, within a month my employer quit woodworking to join the priesthood, leaving me his shop. So there I was with not very many skills and a lot of equipment."

For the next few years, Katherine became a full-time production woodworker, making cribbage boards and yo-yo's. "The work was lucrative, but it was also very monotonous," Katherine remembers. Today, her studio is in Northern California, where she divides her time between small boxes and commissioned furniture. Her work frequently appears in prestigious galleries and craft exhibitions, and has been featured in a number of national publications.

"I respond more to the aesthetic of small things. I like how they look and feel, and they have an intimacy and intricacy that are comfortable for me. I aim for simplicity. What I like best about boxes is that they pretend to be functional, but they're actually very whimsical and decorative."

Coopered Chest

Photo on page 79. Exploded diagram on page 82.

Katherine Heller's name for this cherry and pecan box, her "coopered" chest, comes from the shape of its lid. In the old days, "cooper" was the name given to the artisan who made wood barrels, the universal liquid storage vessel of the pre-industrial age. To fashion the lid, Katherine adapted the cooper's technique of edge joining curved staves. The process of making the lid involves a good deal of reliance on trial and error, so the resulting lid may vary in size from the dimensions given in the materials list. For this reason, it is a good idea to make the lid first, and then size the body to fit it. Like the chest itself, the tray is also dovetailed. The tray divider, with mortised ends that fit into slots dadoed into the sides, is designed to be installed at the time the entire tray is glued up. When complete, the box is given a polished shellac finish.

• To make the lid, first experiment by preparing seven $\frac{3}{8}$"-thick pieces of scrap softwood, each about $5\frac{1}{2}$" long and $\frac{1}{2}$" wide. Using a hand plane, profile the edge of each piece to create an angle slightly less than 90 degrees,

so that when the seven pieces are assembled, they produce the desired barrel curvature. After determining correct angles, repeat the milling procedure using whatever fine hardwood has been selected for the final version. Glue the lid sections. Profile the front and back edges of the lid to the appropriate angle, and use a small hand chisel to cut mortises for the lid, the handle, and the brass lid hinges. Install the lid handle, reinforcing its glue joint with

the three $\frac{1}{16}$-diameter wood dowels shown in the diagram.
• The body of the box is joined together with hand-cut dovetails. Mill a saw kerf dado in the inside face of the front and back to receive Part F, the tray support rails. The edges of the bottom are rabbeted, and fit into a dado on the inside face of the four sides. The curved rabbet in the upper edge of the sides is hand-carved. Test all parts for fit. Finish-sand the interior surfaces, and assemble.

Coopered Chest open

81

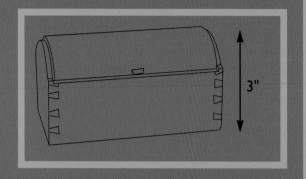

Part	Description	Dimensions	Qty
A	Side	$5/16" \times 2^{11}/16" \times 3"$	2
B	Front/back	$5/16" \times 1^5/16" \times 5^7/16"$	2
C	Bottom	$1/8" \times 2^5/8" \times 5^1/8"$	1
D	Lid	$1/4" \times 3^1/2" \times 5^1/16"$	1
E	Lid handle	$3/16" \times 5/16" \times 5/8"$	1
F	Tray support rail	$1/8" \times 1/8" \times 4"$	2
G	Brass hinge	$3/8" \times 5/8"$	2
H	Tray side	$1/8" \times {15}/16" \times 2^9/16"$	2
J	Tray front/back	$1/8" \times {15}/16" \times 2^3/8"$	2
K	Tray bottom	$1/8" \times 2^1/4" \times 2^3/8"$	1
L	Tray divider	$1/8" \times 3/4" \times 2^1/16"$	1

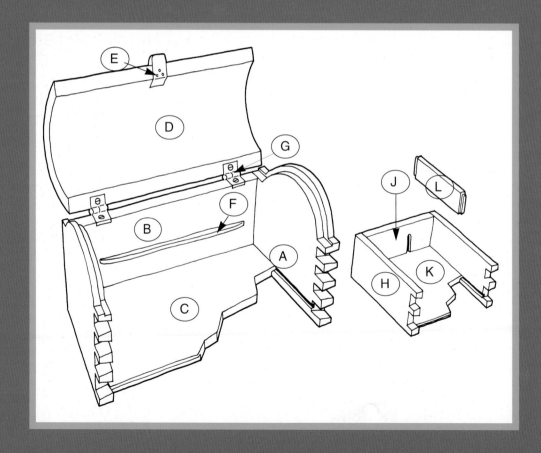

Emily's Chest

Photo on page 83.
Exploded diagram on
page 85.

While Katherine
Heller was making this
box, her daughter
Emily asked if she
could have it to put
her socks in. The
socks didn't fit, but the
name stuck. The body
of this box is European
cherry. The lid panel
and drawer fronts are
spalted pecan.

• Prepare ¼"-thick
stock for the sides,
bottoms, front and
back panel, and mill
the dovetails using a
Japanese hand saw.
Assemble and glue
the box.
• Mill the lid rails, with
their mortise and
tenon ends, and the lid
top panel, and
assemble the lid. Mill
and assemble the
drawers. The drawer
handles are carved by hand,
and a small wedge driven into
a slot in the end of dowel
portion provides a snug fit.

Part	Description	Dimensions	Qty
A	Side	$1/4"$ x $4\,1/8"$ x $4\,5/16"$	2
B	Back panel	$5/16"$ x $7/8"$ x $4\,3/8"$	1
C	Front panel	$1/4"$ x $1\,1/16"$ x $4\,3/8"$	1
D	Bottom	$1/4"$ x $4\,5/26"$ x $5"$	1
E	Drawer separator	$3/16"$ x $3\,7/8"$ x $4\,3/8"$	1
F	Compartment bottom	$1/8"$ x $4\,1/8"$ x $4\,5/8"$	1
G	Lid rail	$1/4"$ x $3/4"$ x $4\,3/4"$	2
H	Lid rail	$1/4"$ x $3/4"$ x $4\,1/4"$	2

Part	Description	Dimensions	Qty
J	Lid top panel	$1/8"$ x $3\,1/8"$ x $3\,1/2"$	1
K	Brass hinge	$3/8"$ x $5/8"$	2
L	Drawer front	$1/4"$ x $1\,5/16"$ x $4\,7/16"$	2
M	Drawer side	$1/4"$ x $1\,1/8"$ x $3\,15/16"$	4
N	Drawer bottom	$3/16"$ x $3\,7/8"$ x $4\,1/16"$	2
O	Drawer back	$1/4"$ x $7/8"$ x $4\,7/16"$	2
P	Drawer handle wedge	$1/16"$ x $1/16"$ x $1/8"$	2
Q	Drawer handle	$5/16"$ x $1/2"$	2
R	Back*	$1/4"$ x $2\,5/16"$ x $4\,3/4"$	1

*(not drawn)

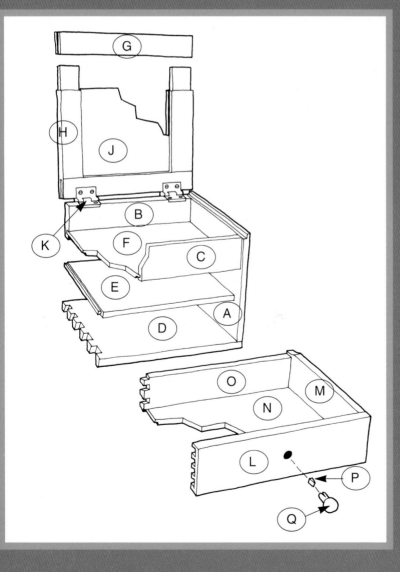

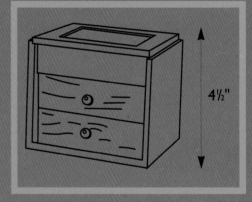

4½"

O'Brien Box

Exploded diagram on page 87.

The idea for this commissioned box, made of natural pearwood, came from Katherine Heller's fascination with the pattern of ebony inlay on the lid. The box begins as a single rectangular solid, 1½" high.

• Prepare stock for the four sides and bottom, which has a feathered edge that sets in a dado. Mill the dovetails using a Japanese hand saw. Assemble and glue the box. Following the instructions on page 14, slice off the lid when the glue is dry.

• Mill slots for the handle (Part H), and the lid alignment rails (Part J), using a $\frac{1}{16}$"-diameter bit on a shaper. Using a series of files, give the five pieces of ebony that make up the lid inlay a pillowed shape. Each piece rests in a shallow chisel-carved depression, whose depth is gauged so that the tops of the ebony pieces are "proud of," or raised slightly above, the surface of the lid.

• Carve and install the lid handle. Give the box a matte spray lacquer finish.

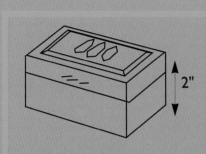

Part	Description	Dimensions	Qty
A	Front/back	$\frac{3}{16}$" x $\frac{15}{16}$" x $2\frac{11}{16}$"	2
B	Side	$\frac{3}{16}$" x $\frac{15}{16}$" x 2"	2
C	Bottom	$\frac{3}{16}$" x $1\frac{3}{4}$" x $2\frac{11}{16}$"	1
D	Lid side	$\frac{3}{16}$" x $\frac{7}{16}$" x 2"	2
E	Lid front/back	$\frac{3}{16}$" x $\frac{7}{16}$" x $2\frac{11}{16}$"	2
F	Lid top panel	$\frac{3}{16}$" x $1\frac{3}{4}$" x $2\frac{1}{2}$"	1
G	Ebony detailing	$\frac{1}{8}$" x $\frac{1}{4}$" x $\frac{1}{4}$" & $\frac{1}{2}$"	5
H	Handle	$\frac{1}{16}$" x $\frac{3}{16}$" x $\frac{3}{4}$"	1
J	Lid alignment rail	$\frac{1}{16}$" x $\frac{1}{8}$" x $1\frac{5}{8}$"	2

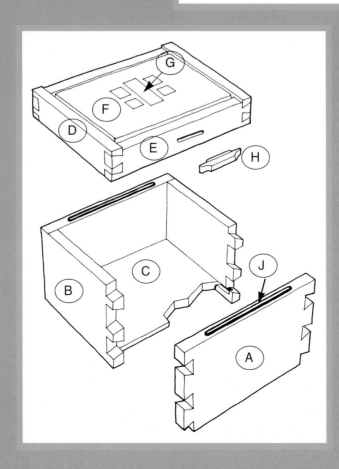

Michael Hamilton & Dee Roberts

Photo by Michael Hamilton

For twenty years, the husband and wife team of Michael Hamilton and Dee Roberts has been making a living in the woodworking realm. After receiving Bachelor of Fine Arts degrees in painting (Dee) and in ceramics (Michael) from the California College of Arts and Crafts, the couple taught ceramics and art classes and operated a pottery and ceramic sculpture studio. Michael also became involved in antique restoration and woodworking.

After moving to Idaho in 1978, both Michael and Dee developed their woodworking skills, and Michael continued to work at restoration and repair. "As a couple in the woodshop, we have a truly synergistic relationship," Michael says. "In our box-making, we don't divide up the tasks. When something needs doing, either of us can do it.

"I've been hooked on boxes for a while now. The last work I did before retiring from clay and moving to wood was small porcelain boxes. I look at the boxes Dee and I make as pieces of furniture, small enough to be held in the hand. We always hope that people who own our boxes will use them to hold something that's close to them in one way or another, whether it's precious or mundane."

Box Elder Burl Box

Photo on page 88. Exploded diagram on page 90.

Although the design and construction of this box, made of box elder and wenge, are straightforward, its makers have enhanced its visual and tactile appeal through subtle hand shaping. The sides of the box are ⅜" thick at the base, but they have been angled by sanding, leaving them only 3/16" thick at the top. The exterior surface of the lid, which is a piece of box elder burl, has been made gently convex.

Box Elder Burl Box open

• Mill and miter the sides, and make a saw kerf dado for the bottom. Finish-sand the interior surfaces, then assemble the box. Mill the edge rails (Part E), and glue them on. Using bits of newspaper, jam the lid in place, and drill holes for the hinge pins. Following the instructions on page 15, install the hinge pins.

• Once the box has been assembled, it can be given its final exterior shape as one piece. Using tape or bits of newspaper, to hold lid closed, sand the four sides and top on the 6" x 48" belt sander to the desired shape and proportions.

• Apply a hand-rubbed oil finish; wax and buff. Following the instructions for Velvet Linings on page 13, line the box with a velvet pad.

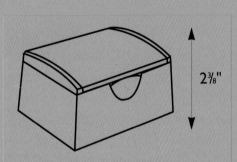

Part	Description	Dimensions	Qty
A	Side	$3/8$" x $1 7/8$" x $4 3/8$"	2
B	Side	$3/8$" x $1 7/8$" x $3 3/8$"	2
C	Bottom	$1/8$" x $2 7/8$" x $3 7/8$	1
D	Lid	$3/8$" x $3 1/8$" x $3 5/8$"	1
E	Edge rails	$3/16$" x $7/16$" x $3 1/8$"	2
F	Hinge pin	$1/16$" x $3/8$"	2

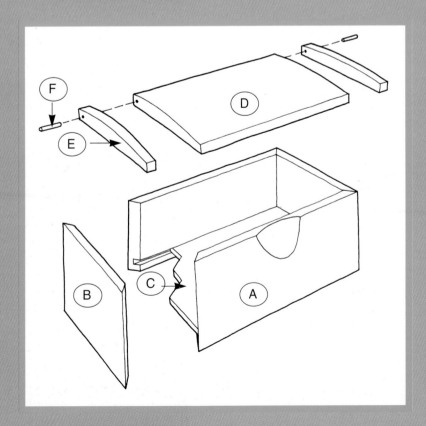

Box on Stilts

Exploded diagram on page 92.

The distinctive shape of this box, with its bracketing legs, can be modified to accommodate any number of proportions, sizes, and wood combinations. This version uses maple and cocobolo.

• Start by milling and assembling the four sides and bottom. *Note: The rabbet across the inside top edge of each side provides a seat for the lid.*

When the glue is dry, gradually taper the outside dimensions of the box, using the 6" x 48" belt sander, so that it becomes narrower at the top.

• To mill the legs, start with two $\frac{5}{16}$"-square rails, each about 10" long. Use the table saw to make the rabbet, then crosscut to final length. Use the drum of a belt sander, or a sanding sleeve on the drill press, to make the curves on the lower portion of each leg. Finish-sand and glue on the legs.

• Mill the handle base (Part E), as a longer rail, then make the saw kerf dado for the handle and crosscut to final size. Part E should sit on a flat surface for proper attachment, so contour the upper surface of the lid (Part D), prior to attaching the handle base.

Part	Description	Dimensions	Qty
A	Side	$\frac{1}{2}$" x $2\frac{1}{8}$" x $4\frac{1}{4}$"	4
B	Bottom	$\frac{1}{8}$" x $1\frac{1}{2}$" x $1\frac{1}{2}$"	1
C	Leg	$\frac{5}{16}$" x $\frac{5}{16}$" x $4\frac{5}{8}$"	4
D	Lid	$\frac{5}{16}$" x $1\frac{9}{16}$" x $1\frac{9}{16}$"	1
E	Handle base	$\frac{5}{16}$" x $\frac{5}{16}$" x $\frac{1}{2}$"	1
F	Handle	$\frac{1}{8}$" x $1\frac{1}{16}$" x $1\frac{5}{8}$"	1

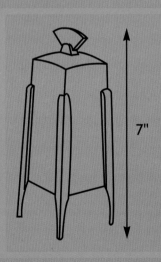

7"

Spline Box

Photo on page 93. Exploded diagram on page 95.

This quilted maple and ebony box is milled using the conventional approach of miter joints and a saw kerf dado for the $\frac{1}{8}$"-plywood bottom. In this design, however, the rabbet in which the lid sits is milled with a router after the box has been glued, so that it will accommodate the rounded edges of the lid. Mill and shape the lid to fit.

• Following the instructions on page 13, make splines or slipfeathers using a jig. Before making the saw cuts for the slipfeathers, angle the saw blade 15 degrees from the vertical. Glue in the slip-feathers. Set the lid in place, held to the box with jammed bits of newspaper. Shape the exterior of the box and lid on the 6" x 48" belt sander.

• Drill for the attachment dowel (Part F).

• The ebony disc that forms the wooden portion of the handle is sliced from a lathe-turned dowel, then sanded to final shape. A second ebony dowel is glued inside the brass tube.

• Apply a hand-rubbed oil finish; wax and buff. Following the instructions for Velvet Linings on page 13, line the box with a velvet pad.

Spline Box open

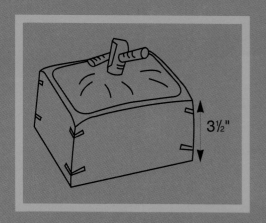

Part	Description	Dimensions	Qty
A	Side	$\frac{7}{16}$" x $2\frac{1}{2}$" x $4\frac{1}{2}$"	2
B	Side	$\frac{7}{16}$" x $2\frac{1}{2}$" x $3\frac{1}{2}$"	2
C	Bottom	$\frac{1}{8}$" x $2\frac{5}{8}$" x $3\frac{5}{8}$"	1
D	Spline	$\frac{1}{8}$" x $\frac{1}{2}$" x 1"	8
E	Lid	$\frac{1}{2}$" x $2\frac{3}{4}$" x $3\frac{3}{4}$"	1
F	Attachment dowel	$\frac{1}{8}$" x $\frac{3}{8}$"	1
G	Handle	$\frac{1}{14}$" diameter x $\frac{3}{8}$"	1
H	Brass tube	$\frac{5}{16}$" x 2"	1
J	Tube filler dowel	$\frac{1}{4}$" x 2"	1

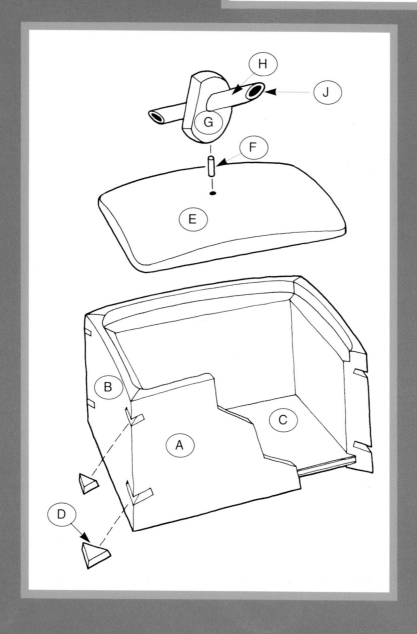

William Chappelow

Photo by Robin Brey

William Chappelow was pursuing a degree in oceanography when he decided to try out a more pioneer-type lifestyle. "As a career, oceanography didn't feel quite right," he remembers, "and I found myself headed into the mountains."

During a winter storm, a massive oak fell in the woods where William was living by Cuyamaca Lake, in the hill country east of San Diego. A few days later, he used a branch from that tree to stir the cauldron in which he was making natural soap. Sitting by the fire that evening, he found himself carving and embellishing the crude piece of oak into his first "spurtle", and as time passed, that tree proved a wellspring of spoons and stirring tools.

William entered into a woodworking partnership with Tom Reed, whose career as a Hollywood record producer also hadn't felt right. "We enjoyed one of those rare artistic partnerships in which each brings out the best in the other," Tom says. "Our skills proved really complementary. William taught me to be an artist, and I taught him how to think in business terms."

The partners gave their utensil enterprise the old English name of Tryyn (pronounced "treen"). Their work has been exhibited in some of the finest galleries in the country, and they have been honored by seeing their pieces purchased for the private collections of British Royalty and United States Presidents.

Double Ladle Box

Photo on page 96. Exploded diagram on page 99.

While most box projects are constructed from sawn or laminated components, this ladle box consists of only two parts, each of them carved and attached with a simple pin hinge.

> Woodworkers share a dedication to ethical self-reliance, responsible entrepreneurship, and self-directed livelihood, all in pursuit of a fundamental spiritual goal: to explore and express our own personal vision. Along the way, we make time to treasure creativity, preserve and strengthen home-based, family based business, and exemplify reverence for conservation of natural materials—not to mention respect for tradition, and the willingness to share our knowledge.
>
> —T.L.

• Start with two solid blocks, maple for the base, 2½" x 4½" x 8½" and California walnut for the lid, 2½" x 4½" x 4½". Use the band saw to rough-out shapes, then carve and finish-sand the lid and base. *Note: William uses small carver's gouges to leave raised ridges on inside surfaces of the box, a technique he refers to as fluting. Because the gouges are so sharp, the surfaces of these ridges are smoother than sanding could produce.*

• Carve the hinge dowel, and use the drill press to drill a hole for the pin. Use a hand-rubbed oil finish, wax, and lots of buffing to bring the exterior surfaces of the base and lid to a high polish, then the insert hinge dowel and tap the pin in place.

Double Ladle Box open

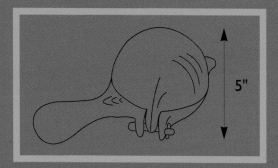

5"

Part	Description	Dimensions	Qty
A	Ladle base	2½" × 4½" × 8½"	1
B	Lid	2½" × 4½" × 4½"	1
C	Hinge dowel	⅜" × 2"	1
D	Pin	⅛" × ⅝"	1

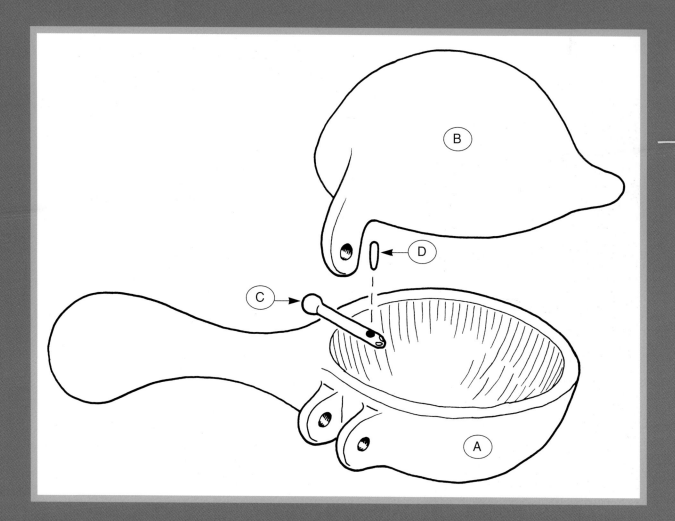

Judy Ditmer

"I knew I was an artist when I was four years old, but it took me a long time to find my medium," Judy Ditmer writes from her Ohio studio. As one of the country's leading woodturners, as well as the author of books on turning bowls and wooden jewelry, Judy's persistence has clearly paid off.

"As a child, I always liked to make things, and to take things apart and figure out how they work. I never got much encouragement, though, even when I went to art school. I'd about given up on being able to do art for a living when I discovered woodturning. I happened to go to a conference on turning, and got just blown out of the water. 'This is it,' I thought to myself, 'this is what I've been looking for.'

"What I like about turning is that the design process and the making process are so integrated. You don't start with a paper-and-pencil drawing, then set out to build it. Instead, you're making decisions as you do the cutting. It's a subtractive process: the result you're after is right there in the wood, waiting. When you reach that pre-existing final form, there's such a sense of rightness."

Tiny Turned Boxes

Photo on page 100.

"When people ask me what these are used for," Judy Ditmer says, "I tell them gold dust, baby teeth, and diamonds—or use your imagination." These tiny boxes, the largest of which stands barely one inch tall, are turned from domestic woods such as lilac, dogwood, and swamp privet, as well as exotics like rosewood, cocobolo, and Brazilian satinwood, which come to Judy as cutoffs from penmakers.

She notes that making small boxes requires more tools than making large ones, and she has a whole set of gouges, which she has custom ground for small work. Since instructions for safe lathe operation are beyond the scope of this book, please consult *The Art of the Lathe* by Patrick Spielman for a comprehensive discussion.

• Using a four-jaw self-centering chuck, first turn a cylinder between centers, then part off the lid. Hollow and finish the inside of lid, and turn a lip on the upper edge of the box. Put the top back on and turn the outside of the box.
• Turn the box inside. When necessary, parts may be wrapped in leather to keep the chuck

from damaging them. The completed boxes are treated with a salad bowl finish made of a mixture of walnut oil and beeswax.

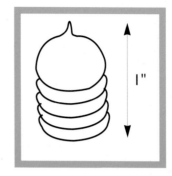

Tiny Turned Box open

Butterfly Boxes

102

Lorenzo Freccia

"Although wood has been my medium of choice, to highlight a beautiful piece of wood, or merely to showcase technique, has never been of great interest to me," writes Lorenzo Freccia from his New England studio. "Instead, I strive for new and imaginative design approaches.

"My greatest satisfaction comes from creating pieces that offer an element of surprise: a box that opens in an unexpected way, or a shape you wouldn't expect to see in wood, or a radically novel design for a familiar object."

Lorenzo was raised and educated in Italy. He emigrated to the United States to attend M.I.T., and after receiving his Bachelor's and Master's degrees, he worked for many years as a chemist and mathematics teacher. He learned traditional joinery techniques during an intensive course of study in furniture making at the Rhode Island School of Design.

Lorenzo has been a full-time designer craftsman since 1986, and his work is exhibited at galleries, museum stores, and shows throughout the country. Lathe-turning has become his specialty; every one of the pieces he makes today is either turned, or contains turned elements.

Butterfly Boxes
Photo on page 102.

The larger box measures 1¼" x 4" x 4¾", and is maple with a walnut top.
• Band saw the box from a block of maple, slice off the bottom, and band saw the interior spaces hollow. Reglue the bottom, and finish-sand the exterior surfaces. Carve the body of the butterfly from a piece of wenge. Glue it on.
• To make the lid, band saw the two pieces of walnut to create the wing shapes. Mill a rabbet in the underside of each so the wings will set in the box.
• Apply a hand-rubbed oil finish to the box and the wings. Use spray flocking to line the interior surfaces of the box.
• Apply 22 carat gold leaf to the exterior surfaces of the wings. Using a fine-pointed tool, create the pattern of veining on the wings by carefully scratching off the gold leaf to reveal the darker walnut beneath.

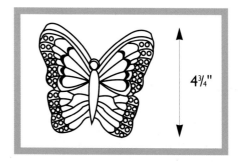

Acorn Box

Photo on page 105.

This acorn box, 1⅝" in diameter and 1½" tall, is made of oak, and houses a pair of tiny acorn-shaped oak earrings. The bottom and lid are turned on the lathe. Since complete instructions for safe lathe operation are beyond the scope of this book, please consult *The Art of the Lathe*

by Patrick Spielman for a comprehensive guide.

Lorenzo has used an engraving pencil to carve a delicate leaf design in the box lid, which is stained dark brown. The ½"-tall earrings are turned from single blocks of oak, and the same dark stain is applied to the upper portion.

A small screw eye is inserted in the end, and brass earring wires are attached.

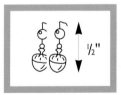

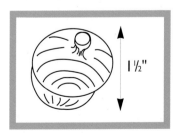

Steve Gray & Kate Noble

Photo by Bob Barrett

Steve Gray and Kate Noble have always had a penchant for the unusual. "I studied photography in school," Steve recalls, "but when I got out of school I started making spinning wheels. Someone asked me to make one, and it wasn't long before I was designing my own. I went on to do cabinetry and furniture, and then for almost ten years I made kaleidoscopes."

Steve became well known for his unusual kaleidoscopes, many of which were sculptural as well as functional. "I like to do sculpture, because it gives me a way to find expression for myself. But for most people, pure sculpture is too hard to focus on. There's a need for some kind of anchor in functionality. The kaleidoscopes were a great way to combine the two."

In addition to spinning wheels and kaleidoscopes, Steve has applied his design and woodworking talents to a variety of boxes, including these screw-top containers. A wooden tea set, made of maple burl and ebony, was featured in one of the books in this woodworking series, *The Art of Elegant Wood Kitchenware.* "I was delighted when someone asked us to make a tea set—that's another form that combines the sculptural with at least the idea of the functional."

Threaded Containers
Photo on page 106.

The dimensions and woods of the four containers are as follows: Largest, with pierced lid: walnut and maple, 2¾" in diameter, 2¼" high. Larger minaret lid: canarywood and padouk, 1⅞" in diameter, 3¾" high. Smaller minaret lid: ebony and tulipwood, ⅞" in diameter, 2¼" high. Smallest: walnut and zebrawood, ⅞" diameter, 2¼" high. The bodies and lids are turned separately on a lathe.

Complete instructions for lathe turning are beyond the scope of this book. Please consult *The Art of the Lathe* by Patrick Spielman for a comprehensive guide.

There are a number of different techniques for producing wooden screw threads. For these containers, Kate Noble uses a treadle metal lathe, a machine made in 1884. Each thread is carefully cut using a small router mounted on the lathe carriage.

The maple insert in the lid of the largest box is made according to a "snowflake construction" technique developed by Steve Gray, and published in *Fine Woodworking Magazine* in 1988, Issue #73. Briefly summarized, the technique involves making six wood wedges, into which a variety of coves, beads, slots, and other details are milled using the router or table saw. These wedges are glued together to form a 2"-diameter dowel, and each snowflake is then sliced off.

To produce the convex surface of the snowflake in this container, Steve glues it into the lid as a flat block, then returns the lid to the lathe and turns the curved profile.

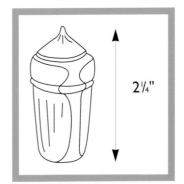

2¼"

Threaded Containers open

John Lavine

Photo by Sharon Siskin

Although he worked as a freelance writer and editor for a time after graduating from Yale as an English major, it wasn't long before John Lavine began building things out of wood. "I was living on a farm in Connecticut," he remembers, "still trying to make a living as a writer, and I built a wooden geodesic dome. At about the same time, I got interested in boat building. Eventually, this interest led me to move to the Pacific Northwest, and in the mid 1970's, I was hired to help rescue and repair a sailboat that had been wrecked in a typhoon off the southern coast of Japan. We flew out there, spent three months rebuilding the boat, and then sailed her back to the West Coast.

"When I got back, I found work doing the detailing and finish carpentry in home remodels. But the real turning point in my career came when I attended a slide talk, given by a Japanese master temple builder, about rebuilding a family shrine using hand tools. I thought it was one of the greatest things I'd ever seen, and I realized that all my creative juices could be satisfied doing something like that."

Now based in Northern California, John teaches, and produces custom furniture from his studio, Kodama Woodworks. A favorite design is his child-size "chalkboard chair," specially painted to allow its owner to draw with chalk, which can be erased.

Reliquary Box

Photo on page 109. Exploded diagram on page 111.

The design of this box, with its through mortise and tenons, wedges, and sliding lid, is based on traditional Japanese proportions and construction techniques. It was made from salvaged old-growth Douglas fir. It shelters a group of wood bones, not shown in the photographs, that are relics of the vanishing North American forests.

• Prepare $\frac{1}{4}$"-thick stock for the sides, top, and bottom. Use a sharp chisel to cut through mortises in the long sides. The tenons on the ends of the short sides can be milled by hand or with a table saw. Use a

hand saw to make a slot in the ends of the tenons, into which the wedges (Part G) will be driven. Finish-sand all parts, and assemble the box. When the glue is dry, sand the sides flush to remove any excess length of the tenon wedges.

• Apply a hand-rubbed oil finish, or use spray lacquer.

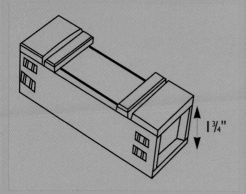

Part	Description	Dimensions	Qty
A	Side	$\frac{1}{4}$" x $1\frac{1}{4}$" x $4\frac{3}{4}$"	2
B	Bottom	$\frac{1}{4}$" x $1\frac{11}{16}$" x $4\frac{3}{4}$"	1
C	Side	$\frac{1}{4}$" x $1\frac{1}{4}$" x $1\frac{11}{16}$"	2
D	Top rail	$\frac{1}{4}$" x $\frac{7}{8}$" x $1\frac{11}{16}$"	2
E	Lid	$\frac{1}{4}$" x $1\frac{3}{16}$" x 3"	1
F	Lid rail	$\frac{1}{4}$" x $\frac{3}{8}$" x $1\frac{11}{16}$"	2
G	Wedge	$\frac{1}{16}$" x $\frac{1}{4}$" x $\frac{1}{4}$"	16

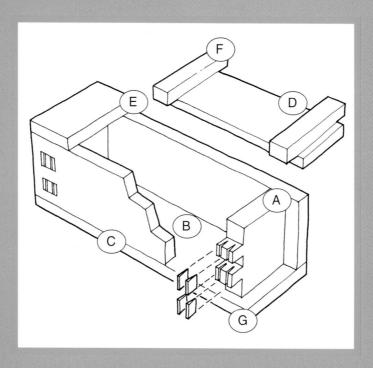

Castle Box

Exploded diagram on page 113.

The body of this figured maple box features interlocking half-lap joints, the ends of which project ¼" beyond the plane of the sides. Before attempting to make a final version, experiment with this joint using pieces of scrap wood.

• Use a dado blade on the table saw to mill slots that go completely through half the width of each side, one on either end. Then lay each side on its face, and using the miter fence, mill the exterior dados, each ¼" deep and ¼" wide.

• Switch to a standard table saw blade, angled at 45 degrees, to complete the interior profile of these dados.

• After carefully adjusting all parts for fit,

finish-sand the interior and exterior surfaces and glue-up the box.

• The lid is made of three pieces of figured maple, edge joined to produce the requisite width. Ebonized walnut was used for the interlocking lid rails (Part D).

• After milling these and trimming the lid to size, use the dado blade to do three additional milling jobs. Make a rabbet on underside of the lid, so it will fit on the box body. Make the four dados on the lid, in which the lid rails sit. Finally, notch each lid rail in two places so the rails will interlock. Finish-sand the parts and assemble the lid.

Note: John uses a spray lacquer finish, and applies black lacquer to the inside of the bottom of the box prior to assembly.

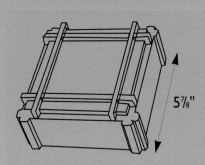

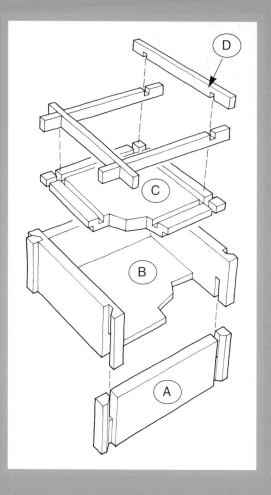

Part	Description	Dimensions	Qty
A	Side	$\frac{1}{2}$" x 2" x 5$\frac{7}{8}$"	4
B	Bottom	$\frac{1}{4}$" x 4$\frac{1}{2}$" x 4$\frac{1}{2}$"	1
C	Lid	$\frac{1}{2}$" x 4$\frac{7}{8}$" x 4$\frac{7}{8}$"	1
D	Interlocking lid rail	$\frac{1}{4}$" x $\frac{1}{2}$" x 5$\frac{1}{2}$"	4

Joel Gelfand

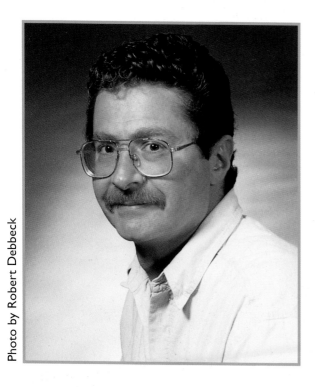

After earning a bachelor's and a master's degree in fine arts, Joel Gelfand decided to dedicate himself to bringing art education to urban youth, and got a job teaching sixth-, seventh-, and eighth-grade art in the South Bronx borough of New York City.

He writes, "My ten years as an art teacher taught me a lot about what it means to kids to take their own ideas seriously. I never found out what became of most of my students except for one kid, who made it as a major league baseball player. But I like to think that maybe some of what I taught them enriched their lives as much as the experience enriched mine.

"When it came time for me to move on to something else, woodworking seemed the obvious thing to do, since it runs in my family."

Joel's father was a woodworker, as were his grandfather and his grandfather's six brothers. Family legend has it that the tradition may be several generations older than that.

Joel has added fifteen years to that tradition by designing and handcrafting furniture in his New York studio, not far from the South Bronx where he once taught. The miniature chest featured here is his first small-scale piece. "I'm going to go in the direction of making little things," Joel says. "They take as much time as big things, but they're more fun."

Miniature Chest

Photo on page 114. Exploded diagram on page 117.

This tiny chest has free-form door panels of maple burl, whose voids have been filled with a mixture of turquoise dust and epoxy. The door rails are ebony. The body of the chest is made of cocobolo, and it sits on a wenge base. The drawer fronts are African vermilion.

• To make the box body, begin by rabbeting the front edge of the two ⅝"-thick sides (Part A). This will allow the drawer fronts to close flush. Mill the three ¼" dados ¼" deep in each side; the ¼"-plywood drawer bottoms, extending beyond either side of each drawer as glides, will run in these dados. *Note: In the list of materials, dimensions are given for the bottom drawer only. Size the other two drawers as needed.*
• Mill the back and the miters on the top, bottom, and sides, and assemble. Mill the base. To raise the chest slightly above its base, make two ¼"-deep saw kerf dados (not shown in the

drawing) in the underside of the bottom, running from front to back approximately four inches apart. Glue the base riser rail (Part Q) into each. Glue the chest onto the base.

• Each door has only two rails, and the 1/4"-thick free-form maple door panels fit into a shallow dado milled in the edge of each. After assembling the doors, drill holes for the hinge pins in both doors and in the two 5/16"-thick rails (Part D). Make a test assembly to be certain everything fits, then glue on the top and bottom rails along with the doors and the hinge pins.

• For drawers, first mill pieces of 1/4" plywood for bottoms. Assemble the drawer sides and fronts after their interior surfaces have been finish-sanded; these simply sit atop each drawer bottom. The placement of drawer handles will vary depending on the shape of the freeform maple door panels; locate them appropriately, then install the handles.

• After final sanding, oil and wax the exterior surfaces. Following the instructions for Velvet Linings on page 13, line each drawer with a velvet pad.

Miniature Chest open

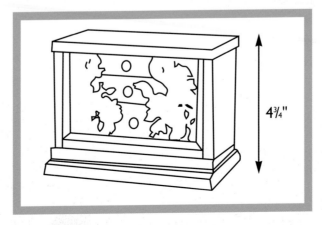

4³⁄₄"

Part	Description	Dimensions	Qty
A	Side	$\frac{5}{8}$" x $3\frac{1}{4}$" x 4"	2
B	Top/bottom	$\frac{5}{16}$" x $3\frac{1}{4}$" x $5\frac{5}{8}$"	2
C	Back	$\frac{1}{8}$" x $5\frac{7}{16}$" x $3\frac{3}{4}$"	1
D	Door top & bottom rail	$\frac{5}{16}$" x $\frac{11}{16}$" x $5\frac{5}{8}$"	2
E	Base	$\frac{3}{8}$" x $4\frac{1}{2}$" x 6"	1
F	Vertical door rail	$\frac{3}{8}$" x $\frac{1}{2}$" x $2\frac{3}{4}$"	2
G	Horizontal door rail	$\frac{3}{8}$" x $\frac{1}{2}$" x $2\frac{3}{4}$"	2
H	Freeform door panel	$\frac{1}{4}$" x 2" x $2\frac{3}{4}$"	2

J	Brass hinge pin	$\frac{1}{16}$" x $\frac{1}{2}$"	4
K	Lower drawer front	$\frac{1}{8}$" x $1\frac{7}{16}$" x $4\frac{5}{8}$"	1
L	Lower drawer side	$\frac{1}{4}$" x $\frac{13}{16}$" x $2\frac{3}{4}$"	2
M	Lower drawer back	$\frac{1}{4}$" x $\frac{13}{16}$" x $3\frac{3}{8}$"	1
N	Lower drawer bottom	$\frac{1}{4}$" x 3" x $4\frac{1}{8}$"	1
O	Drawer handle pin	$\frac{1}{16}$" x $\frac{1}{2}$"	3
P	Drawer handle	$\frac{3}{8}$" diameter x $\frac{1}{4}$"	3
Q	Base riser rail*	$\frac{1}{8}$" x $\frac{3}{8}$" x $4\frac{3}{4}$"	2

*not drawn

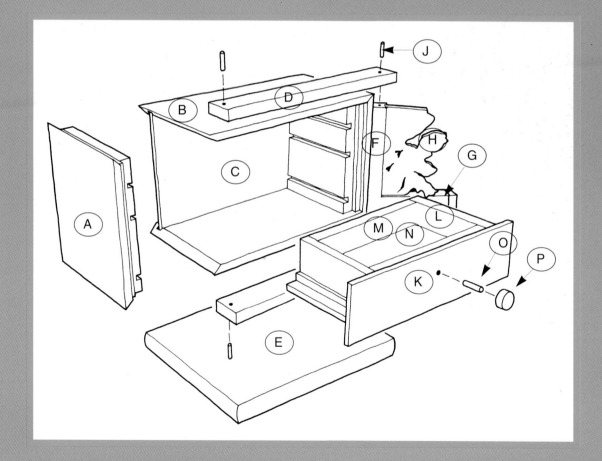

Chapter Two: Gallery

Flared Openwork Vessel

Dewey Garrett

Although he was trained as an engineer, Dewey Garrett took up the lathe to develop his woodworking skills for cabinetry and furniture. "I found the process so stimulating that woodturning has become a dedicated pursuit," says Dewey. "Converting a featureless block of wood into a graceful, symmetrical form is always fascinating, and full of surprises.

"While I'm at work on the lathe, all the details and color of the object are integrated into a spinning blur, that reveals only its outline. At rest, the same object shows complex details and dramatic color, and never loses its sense of motion."

A self-taught turner who makes or modifies many of the tools he uses, Dewey's turnings often appear in national and international exhibitions. He describes his current work as a search for ways to expose and combine turned shapes into new and unexpected compositions. "The mechanics of the lathe produce a simplicity and a symmetry, and the turnings I'm doing now continue to explore how these factors constrain the structure of forms."

Flared Openwork Vessel

Photo on page 118.

Dewey's turnings explore ways to create unusual shapes, and then recombine them into unexpected forms. The elaborate architecture of this tiny box, $2\frac{5}{8}$" tall, is the product of a careful sequence of turning, carving, cutting, and reassembly.

Flared Openwork Vessel open

Banksia Pod Box

This exquisite vessel is 2½" in diameter and 2¾" tall, to the tip of its lift-off lid. The turner has left in place the voids that naturally form in the pods of this tree.

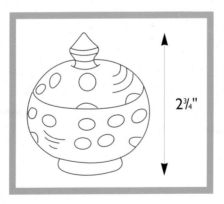

2¾"

Flared Openwork Vessel

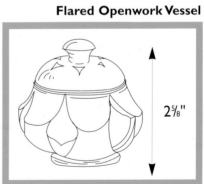

2⅝"

Bonnie Klein

"I turn for the love of the creative process," writes Bonnie Klein from her studio in Renton, Washington. "I am addicted to discovery, progress, and the fact that perfection is forever elusive. But as I strive for it, yesterday's challenges become the basic skills of tomorrow." Best known for turning miniatures, she also turns lidded containers, bowls, and many other small scale projects, such as replacement spindles for antique and furniture restorers.

Bonnie has travelled all over the United States, Canada, England, Ireland, and Australia, demonstrating her woodturning techniques and conducting workshops. "I love to travel, and share my enthusiasm for turning with others. I especially enjoy working with young people, because I fear they are losing the opportunity to learn woodworking skills in school."

Her interest in sharing her knowledge and advancing the art of ornamental turning has led Bonnie to design and manufacture a specialized lathe for small turnings. She also produces a line of woodturning tools, and a lathe attachment for milling screw threads, as well as series of instructional videotapes.

Bone Box
Photo on page 121.

This delicate box, with its threaded lid, is 1¾" in diameter, and stands 2" tall. "I used to make boxes from ivory, which has been the substance of choice for turning for centuries. Now that ivory is no longer available, I work with bone," Bonnie writes. The flared profile of the vessel is complemented by a five-petal rose design on surface of the lid.

Bone, Blackwood, and Mopane Box
Photo on page 121.

Standing 1⅞" tall, with a diameter of 2¼", the body and threaded lid of this box were turned from a single piece of mopane wood. A narrow blackwood ring on the lid surrounds a central circular inset of bone decorated with an incised floral design.

Bone, Black-wood, and Cocobolo Box

Photo on page 121.

"I've been experimenting with turnings of cow bone, which I get from the local butcher shop," says Bonnie Klein. "I boil and bleach the bones, and they make an excellent substitute for ivory." This box is $2\frac{3}{4}$" in diameter, and stands $2\frac{3}{8}$" tall. The surface of the threaded blackwood lid features a continuous pattern of marks called chatterwork or enginework.

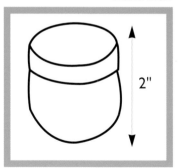

Bone Box

2"

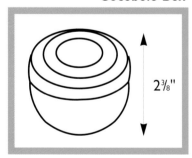

Bone, Blackwood, and Cocobolo Box

$2\frac{3}{8}$"

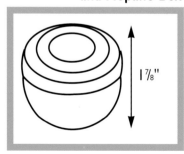

Bone, Blackwood, and Mopane Box

$1\frac{7}{8}$"

Doug Finkel

Doug Finkel has just completed the transition from part-time to full-time woodworker, having given up his job teaching high school woodworking to concentrate on furniture and boxes. "My traditional furniture focuses on subtle curves and proportions," Doug writes from his newly-equipped Virginia shop, "but I like the spontaneous quality of these creature boxes. I'm toying with the idea of incorporating some of my creature designs into tables, lamps and clocks."

Doug graduated from college with a degree in creative writing, but soon turned to carpentry to support himself. "While I was building houses I received a commission for a table, and it turned out so well I decided to enroll in a two-year woodworking program to develop my skills. That was one of the best decisions I've made in my life.

"I've always thought that turners place too much emphasis on the vessel," Doug says. "My rocking eyeball boxes get away from that, yet they're not traditional boxes either. The inspiration for them came from cartoons. Things can happen and exist in cartoons that wouldn't be possible in real life. I can do things with characters that no director could ever do with a live actor. The best thing about the eyeballs is how much fun they were. I just laughed and laughed the whole time I was making them."

Rocking Eyeball Boxes
Photo on page 124.

Designed to hold a small piece of jewelry or a special keepsake, these eyeball boxes are made of maple, cocobolo, ebony, vermilion, dyed maple, and mixed media. They are 2½" in diameter, and stand 4" high. Each is attached to a base carved like a cartoon character's foot. The attachment is made using a coiled spring, which allows the eyeball to rock.

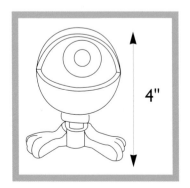

Bill McDowell

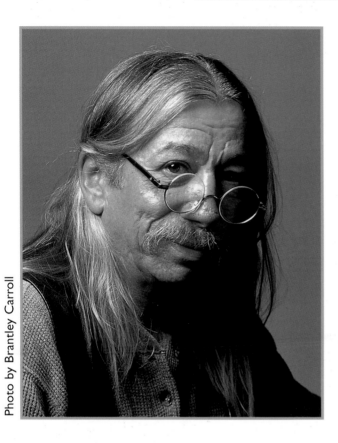

"These designs are very distinctive, and it's interesting how people respond to them. My signature latch mechanism, for example, seems to evoke images from science fiction, particularly the Starship Enterprise. I'm not really sure myself where the inspiration comes from, so I guess anyone's interpretation is both a little bit right and a little bit wrong."

Like many box makers, Bill is a graduate of seventh-grade woodshop who went on to study industrial and product design in college. "In my boxes, I emphasize crisp lines, and linear, almost metallic forms. When it comes to furniture, though, I go out of my way to incorporate the wood's natural splits, gnarls, and rotten spots. That's why wood is my medium: it's the only material where high-tech and organic are equally at home."

"I started a production shop with a partner about twenty years ago," Bill McDowell writes, "and we were quite successful. 'Wood Goods', as we called our enterprise, ran a fairly large shop, with several full-time employees, and forty to fifty galleries carried our work nationwide. After a while, though, it was time for me to go off in my own direction."

That direction turned out to include furniture and a series of boxes and clocks that Bill calls "Art Tekno-Deco." In this continually evolving, five year progression, Bill explores his fascination with juxtaposing the organic and the manufactured, the mechanical and the sensual, the practical and the sublime.

Design is what, for practical purposes, can be conveyed in words and by drawing: workmanship is what, for practical purposes, cannot. In practice the designer hopes the workmanship will be good, but the workman decides whether it shall be good or not. On the workman's decision depends a great part of the quality of our environment.
—David Pye, *The Nature and Art of Workmanship,* Cambridge Press, 1968

Single Ring Box and Double Necklace Box

Photo on page 126.

Standing 4" high, the smaller box is made from bloodwood, quartersawn wenge, and curly maple. "I call this one my single ring box," Bill writes from his studio in upstate New York. "When I'm making it for a divorcee's ring, I call it my single ring casket."

The Double Necklace Box, 3¼" tall and 6½" long, is made of Nicaraguan rosewood, quartersawn wenge, and curly maple. Like many of Bill's boxes, both of the pieces in the photograph include a spring-loaded mechanism that must be squeezed to release the latch.

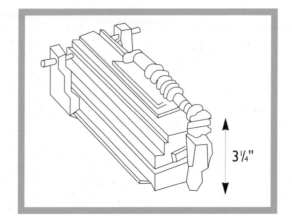

3¼"

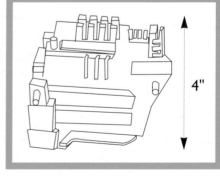

4"

Michael Mode

Photo by Lighting Photo Studio

"I've spent many years learning the skills of wood turning and running a woodworking business," says Michael Mode. "Now I'm fortunate to be at that wonderful point where I'm continually excited about making something new. I want to make as many things as I possibly can while I'm still on the planet. As I've become more successful as an artist, I can make pieces that are extremely creative and far-out, and still feel reasonably sure that the market will support me."

Michael's woodworking career began with turned ornaments, but as he sought ways to change and evolve his work, he turned for inspiration to the travels he had made through India some 20 years earlier. He was fascinated with the styles and aesthetics of the Mogul Emperors, whose reign left monuments throughout India, best known of which is the

Taj Mahal. The first fruits of this evolution were his "winged vessels," a series of turned pieces that had a certain alien aspect. The comments of people who saw them referred to oriental temples, undersea creatures, and—especially—spacecraft from other worlds.

Since then, the work Michael produces in his New England studio has won award after award, and has entered leading private and public collections, including the American Craft Museum, and the Yale University Art Gallery. "I've learned how to be a conduit for my own inspiration," he adds. "It's such a privilege to be able to make your livelihood from that."

Miniature Chess Set Box

Photo on page 129.

Led always by his intuition and a fondness for discovery and chance, Michael's career as a turner has been a steady evolution toward more and more extraordinary work. "Like a lot of things I do," he says, "this miniature chess set came about as the result of a whim. I had been making standard sized sets, based on an eighteenth-century French design I liked, when I was asked to be part of a gallery show on miniature turnings."

In the resulting set, the lacewood, ebony, Indian rosewood, and holly vessel is 6" high and 8½" in diameter. The turned pieces, of ebony and tagua nut, are ⅜" to ¾" tall. To facilitate handling of men so small, the artist has included tweezers, custom-made of Indian rosewood.

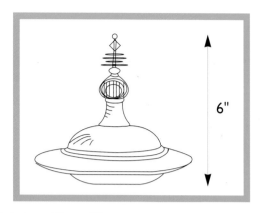

6"

Miniature Chess Pieces

Miniature Chess Tweezers

Miniature Chess Set Box open

David Sengel

Photo by Winters

"I played a lot of piano from the time I was seven until about thirteen," says David Sengel, "and my dad had a woodshop. When I got out of college, I combined music and wood by repairing and restoring pianos, which involves quite a bit of woodwork. Then one day, I ordered a cheap lathe out of a catalog, and my interest developed from there."

What inspired David to pursue his career as a turner, however, was a series of classes he took with master woodturners. "I was dabbling in woodwork as a hobby, and that kind of overlapped with my piano business for several years. But those classes were the kick that really got me into turning. After I saw what could be done, I decided to push it as hard as I could."

In 1991, David began a series of turned and constructed pieces that featured thorns.

"I'm interested in other parts of the tree besides lumber, as well as in organic shapes and materials generally, and I've always been a junk hound. A fellow turner sent me a box of Arkansas locust thorns, and once I had them, I figured I'd better do something with them. Now I use rose, blackberry and trifoliate orange thorns as well as locust.

"I've had fun with the thorn pieces, and they've certainly helped make my reputation, but the thorns are tedious to match and to apply, and they get all over my shop. I'm about ready for something new."

Spider Box
Photo on page 132.

David Sengel's interest in animal and insect forms began when he observed a master woodturner doing multi-axis work. In the spider box, which stands 3½" tall, several of the legs are single pieces of locust branch, selected for their appropriate shape. Each leg is doweled into the body for strength. Arkansas honey locust thorns adorn the body, which is hollowed out to create a container.

Thorn Box
Photo on page 135.

The small lidded box is 3¼" in diameter, and stands 2½" tall. Attached to its underside are five perfect rose thorns, which serve as feet. The Spider Box and Thorn Box are coated with black spray lacquer.

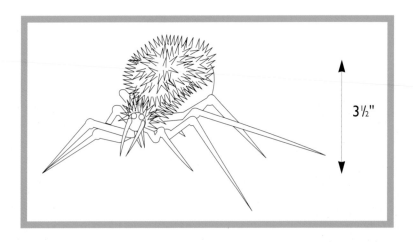

3½"

Spider Box open

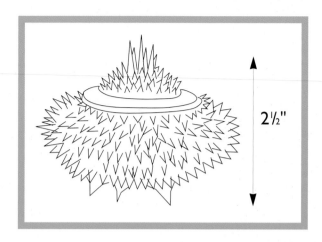

2½"

Thorn Box

Po Shun Leong

Born and educated in England, Po Shun Leong received a scholarship to study in France with Le Corbusier, one of the pioneers of modern architecture. After graduating with honors from the London Architectural Association, he moved to Mexico, where he lived for fifteen years, working as a designer and absorbing the local culture.

After moving to Southern California in 1981, Leong began creating a series of boxes. "My boxes are really architecture on a small scale. I do plans as if they were buildings, with floors and a roof." Drawing on Mexican, classical Greek, and Gothic design, Po Shun infuses each piece with what he terms "oriental complexity." These and related architectural traditions serve as sources for the columns, stairways, arches, bridges and other elements that his boxes combine in such novel ways.

Leong's cabinets, jewelry chests, furniture, and sculptures are widely exhibited and avidly collected around the world. He will be the subject of a forthcoming volume in this series of woodworking books by Tony Lydgate, published by Sterling/Chapelle.

Imagined City
Photo on page 137.

The woods in this hinged-lid box, which stands 12¾" tall, and has a base diameter of 8", include purpleheart, buckeye burl, holly, pau amarillo, mahogany, maple, ebony, pink ivorywood, pernambuco, tulipwood, wenge, cocobolo, cherry burl, bocote, and palm. The upper portion, with its terraces, towers, pavilions and platforms, swings open on a wooden pin hinge to reveal an inner sanctum.

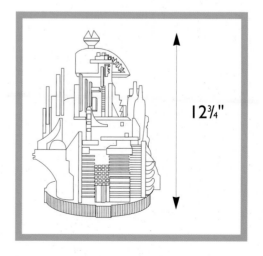

12¾"

ed City Open close-up

Imagined City open

Christopher Cantwell

It is unusual for a woodworker to work at a professional level while still in high school, but Christopher Cantwell sold his first piece of furniture, an ash dining table, when he was only 15. Three years before that, he won the Young Masters competition at the Central California Art League.

Mostly self-taught, Christopher educated himself by reading books and articles on woodworking, and by studying every wooden object he could find to see how it was made. After a career detour that included construction work, cabinetmaking, guitar building, and becoming a world-class rock climber, Christopher returned full time to his first love.

Most of his work involves one-of-a-kind elements that harmonize with the character of the many different species of wood he uses.

"I like to design with the actual pieces of wood," Christopher says. "Things like the shape of a box leg, or how to place inlays within the flow of the grain—these create a dialogue between me and the wood."

His current work is divided among boxes, wall art, and furniture commissions, particularly for conference and dining room tables. All are well represented in major collections, including the White House. Christopher and his unique style are frequently the subject of newspaper and magazine articles.

Imagination Box

Photo on page 140.

The hinged-lid box base of this carved, constructed, and turned fantasy sculpture stands about 5" tall. Its detachable spires—each of which conceals a hidden compartment—rise to 12". The sides of the sculpture are ziricote, carefully selected to show light-colored sapwood. The flowing, organic lids are cocobolo. Other woods include narra, pink ivorywood, lignum vitae, bocote, ebony,

Imagination Box close-up

Honduras rose-wood, granadillo, kingwood, satin-wood, birdseye maple, and figured walnut. The intricate laminated and marquetry inlays, visible on the front of the box, and some of the spires, are custom made.

"This is the latest in an evolving series of boxes I've done," the artist says. "It definitely has the feeling of a cityscape, and I was imagining something futuristic, something floating out there in space. While making it, I tried to distill my ideas down to their essential elements—so with all its little secret hiding places, I think of this as a vessel for keeping gemstones, rather than finished jewelry."

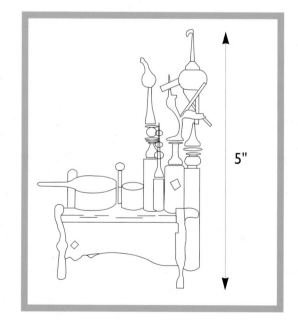

5"

Metric Equivalency Chart

mm-millimetres   cm-centimetres
inches to millimetres and centimetres

inches	mm	cm	inches	cm	inches	cm
1/8	3	0.3	9	22.9	30	76.2
1/4	6	0.6	10	25.4	31	78.7
1/2	13	1.3	12	30.5	33	83.8
5/8	16	1.6	13	33.0	34	86.4
3/4	19	1.9	14	35.6	35	88.9
7/8	22	2.2	15	38.1	36	91.4
1	25	2.5	16	40.6	37	94.0
1 1/4	32	3.2	17	43.2	38	96.5
1 1/2	38	3.8	18	45.7	39	99.1
1 3/4	44	4.4	19	48.3	40	101.6
2	51	5.1	20	50.8	41	104.1
2 1/2	64	6.4	21	53.3	42	106.7
3	76	7.6	22	55.9	43	109.2
3 1/2	89	8.9	23	58.4	44	111.8
4	102	10.2	24	61.0	45	114.3
4 1/2	114	11.4	25	63.5	46	116.8
5	127	12.7	26	66.0	47	119.4
6	152	15.2	27	68.6	48	121.9
7	178	17.8	28	71.1	49	124.5
8	203	20.3	29	73.7	50	127.0

yards to metres

yards	metres	yards	metres	yards	metres	yards	metres	yards	metres
1/8	0.11	2 1/8	1.94	4 1/8	3.77	6 1/8	5.60	8 1/8	7.43
1/4	0.23	2 1/4	2.06	4 1/4	3.89	6 1/4	5.72	8 1/4	7.54
3/8	0.34	2 3/8	2.17	4 3/8	4.00	6 3/8	5.83	8 3/8	7.66
1/2	0.46	2 1/2	2.29	4 1/2	4.11	6 1/2	5.94	8 1/2	7.77
5/8	0.57	2 5/8	2.40	4 5/8	4.23	6 5/8	6.06	8 5/8	7.89
3/4	0.69	2 3/4	2.51	4 3/4	4.34	6 3/4	6.17	8 3/4	8.00
7/8	0.80	2 7/8	2.63	4 7/8	4.46	6 7/8	6.29	8 7/8	8.12
1	0.91	3	2.74	5	4.57	7	6.40	9	8.23
1 1/8	1.03	3 1/8	2.86	5 1/8	4.69	7 1/8	6.52	9 1/8	8.34
1 1/4	1.14	3 1/4	2.97	5 1/4	4.80	7 1/4	6.63	9 1/4	8.46
1 3/8	1.26	3 3/8	3.09	5 3/8	4.91	7 3/8	6.74	9 3/8	8.57
1 1/2	1.37	3 1/2	3.20	5 1/2	5.03	7 1/2	6.86	9 1/2	8.69
1 5/8	1.49	3 5/8	3.31	5 5/8	5.14	7 5/8	6.97	9 5/8	8.80
1 3/4	1.60	3 3/4	3.43	5 3/4	5.26	7 3/4	7.09	9 3/4	8.92
1 7/8	1.71	3 7/8	3.54	5 7/8	5.37	7 7/8	7.20	9 7/8	9.03
2	1.83	4	3.66	6	5.49	8	7.32	10	9.14

Index